# كتاب الأخلاق والسير

# *Al-Akhlaq wa Al-Siyar*

## Morals And Behaviours

Ibn Hazm al-Andalusi

Translated by
Shaykh Dr. Muhammad Abū Laylah

Dar Ul Thaqafah

**Dar ul Thaqafah**
www.darulthaqafah.com
https://twitter.com/darulthaqafah

*Find our titles on your favorite online bookstore using the keyword 'Dar Ul Thaqafah'.*

2023 CE – 1444 H

## Translation of the Qur'ān

It should be perfectly clear that the Qur'ān is only authentic in its original language, Arabic. Since perfect translation of the Qur'ān is impossible, we have used the translation of the meaning of the Qur'ān throughout the book, as the result is only a crude meaning of the Arabic text.

Qur'ānic verses appear in speech marks proceeded by a reference to the Surah and verse number. Sayings (*Hadith*) of Prophet Muhammad (saw) appear in inverted commas along with reference to the Hadith Book and its Reporter.

Ibn Ḥazm رحمه الله dedicated his book to the benefit of all mankind.

Here I follow his example in dedicating this book to all my fellow men, particularly to the very rich, who are in danger of forgetting life's true values, and to the very poor, who may not realise that they can be rich in the things that matter. Money is not everything, there are greater treasures available for all.

The world is for everybody, but heaven is only for the pure in heart, the virtuous, and most pious.

— Shaykh Dr. Muḥammad Abū Laylah, *In Pursuit of Virtue*

يَلُوحُ الْخَطُّ فِي القِرْطَاسِ دَهْرًا
وَكَاتِبُهُ رَمِيمٌ فِي التُّرَابِ

*Writing shines on paper for an eon,*
*while its writer has decayed in the earth.*

We thank the family of Shaykh Dr. Muḥammad Abū Laylah رحمه الله for granting permission to release this work as *ṣadaqah jāriyah*. May Allāh (سبحانه وتعالى) accept from us our good deeds and forgive us our shortcomings, and may He (سبحانه وتعالى) make this work beneficial for the Muslims.

# TRANSLITERATION KEY

| | | | | | | |
|---|---|---|---|---|---|---|
| ء | ’(1) | ر | r(6) | ف | f |
| ا | ā, a | ز | z | ق | q(13) |
| ب | b | س | s | ك | k |
| ت | t | ش | sh | ل | l |
| ث | th(2) | ص | ṣ(7) | م | m |
| ج | j | ض | ḍ(8) | ن | n |
| ح | ḥ(3) | ط | ṭ(9) | ه | h(14) |
| خ | kh(4) | ظ | ẓ(10) | و | ū, u, w |
| د | d | ع | ʿ(11) | ي | ī, i, y |
| ذ | dh(5) | غ | gh(12) | | |

1. A distinctive glottal stop made at the bottom of the throat.
2. Pronounced like the *th* in *think*.
3. Hard *h* sound made at the Adam's apple in the middle of the throat.
4. Pronounced like *ch* in Scottish *loch*.
5. Pronounced like *th* in *this*.
6. A slightly trilled *r* made behind the upper front teeth.
7. An emphatic *s* pronounced behind the upper front teeth.
8. An emphatic *d*-like sound made by pressing the entire tongue against the upper palate.
9. An emphatic *t* sound produced behind the front teeth.
10. An emphatic *th* sound, like the *th* in this, made behind the front teeth.
11. A distinctive Semitic sound made in the middle of the throat and sounding to a Western ear more like a vowel than a consonant.
12. A guttural sound made at the top of the throat resembling the untrilled German and French *r*.
13. A hard *k* sound produced at the back of the palate.
14. This sound is like the English *h* but has more body. It is made at the very bottom of the throat and pronounced at the beginning, middle, and ends of words.

# *Editor's Note*

All praise belongs to Allāh, Lord of all the worlds. May peace and blessings be upon our Prophet Muḥammad, upon his family, his companions, and all those who follow his guidance until the Day of Judgment.

This PDF file is a translation of Ibn Ḥazm's رحمه الله book *Kitāb al-akhlāq wa al-siyar fī mudāwat al-nufūs*. Its content is from Archive.org. It was originally the last part of the book *In Pursuit of Virtue* by Shaykh Muḥammad Abū Laylah رحمه الله published in 1990 by Ta-Ha Publishers. This work is not commercial and is only meant to promote the legacy of Ibn Ḥazm رحمه الله.

I edited the source used for this document. Some points didn't flow well in English and were edited. Others were compared with the original Arabic and edited accordingly; these are discussed in the footnotes. I replaced the term "God" with "Allāh" throughout. I added the Arabic for Quran *āyāt*; these are to be read right-to-left even if split across two lines. I added footnotes of word definitions from the Oxford English Dictionary, 2nd ed. With the exception of these, all other footnotes are preceded by a symbol (✿) to differentiate them from the original translator's footnotes. I removed footnotes regarding the translator's comparison of the Arabic to a French translation as well as discussions regarding different editions and manuscripts since these would not benefit the common reader in English; anyone interested in these should resort to the edition by Ta-Ha Publishers. Please note that the paragraph numbers are originally there in the original Arabic edition used by the translator – as per my understanding – to facilitate referencing; some editions of the book do not have them. The translator carried them over into his translation probably for the same reason. This means that two or three subsequent points can be from the same expression of thought.

The following sources were referenced:

[A] *Risālah fī mudāwāh al-nufūs wa tahdhīb al-akhlāq* (Egypt: Nile Print-
ers, AH 1323),
[B] *Kitāb al-akhlāq wa al-siyar* (Beirut: Dār Ibn Ḥazm, n.d.),
[C] *Kitāb al-akhlāq wa al-siyar* (Beirut: al-Lajnah al-Duwalīyah li-tarjamat
al-rawā'i', 1961),
[D] *Rasā'il Ibn Ḥazm* (Beirut: Mu'assasah al-'Arabiyyah li al-dirāsāt wa
al-nashr, 2nd Ed. 1987), and
[E] *In Pursuit of Virtue* (UK: Ta-Ha Publishers, 1990).

I would like to thank Abū Khuzaymah of Salafi Research Institute (UK)
for giving me permission to use the brief biography of Ibn Ḥazm رحمه الله he
had compiled. In relation to this, special thanks go to Zahraa Lotfi for suggestions with regard to punctuation, style, and grammar. I would also like
to acknowledge Zahid Mateen, Bukhari, Ustādh Sajaad, Hamza Peer, and
Abdul Rehman Memoni for their editorial and translation suggestions.

If you find any mistakes or editorial errors in this work, please contact me.
May Allāh accept our efforts and rectify our souls.

Mohammad Khalid Hussain
mohammad.khalid.hussain@gmail.com
Telegram: KhalidHussain
Dār al-Iḥsān, Malaysia
20 Jumādá al-Ūlá 1444

*About the Translator*

Shaykh Dr. Muḥammad Abū Laylah رحمه الله was born in 1942 in a village in the Qalyubia Governorate, slightly north of Cairo, Egypt. He graduated from Al-Azhar University and went on to lecture in its Faculty of Theology from 1970–5, specialising in Da‘wah and Comparative Religion. He subsequently prepared a doctoral thesis on Comparative Religion at the University of Exeter entitled *Ibn Ḥazm on Jews and Judaism*, which was accepted in 1984, and which led to his collaboration in the publication of *Faith meets Faith* (London, Institute of Higher Education, 1988).

Some of the Shaykh's publications include *al-Ḥiwār fī al-Qur'ān* (Dialogue in the Quran), *The Story of Joseph (Yusuf) (Peace be upon him) in the Qur'ān*, *al-Qur'ān al-Karīm min al-manẓar al-ishtishrāqī* (The Glorious Quran from the Orientalists' point of view) and *The Qur'ān and the Gospels*. He also served as the head of the Department of English and Literature under the Faculty of Languages and Translation at Al-Azhar University, and was also a member of the Supreme Islamic Council of Egypt. The Shaykh's incisive scholarship produced many influential articles and established him as an authoritative speaker in universities and institutes throughout Europe.

Shaykh Dr. Muḥammad Abū Laylah رحمه الله breathed his last in June 2021. He is survived by his wife and four children. May Allāh accept from him his good deeds and forgive his shortcomings. Āmīn!

[Content was taken from the blurb on the back cover of Ta-Ha Publication's *In Pursuit of Virtue* and the Shaykh's curriculum vitae.]

# *A Brief Biography of Ibn Ḥazm*

## Name, genealogy, and ancestry

His *kunyah* is Abū Muḥammad and his full name and lineage is ʿAlī ibn Aḥmad ibn Saʿīd ibn Ḥazm ibn Ghālib ibn Ṣāliḥ ibn Khalaf ibn Maʿdān ibn Sufyān ibn Yazīd. His forefather, Yazīd, was a freed slave of Yazīd ibn Abī Sufyān, and of Persian ancestry. His forefather, Khalaf, was the first from the family who entered al-Andalus while his grandfather, Saʿīd ibn Ḥazm, moved to Qurṭubah (Córdoba) from Lablah (Niebla). His father Abū ʿAmr Aḥmad ibn Saʿīd, was considered to be a learned, cultured, and honest man; he was also an expert in the Arabic language and served as a vizier for the viceroys al-Manṣūr Muḥammad ibn Abī ʿĀmir and his son, ʿAbd al-Malik al-Muẓaffar.

Ibn Ḥazm رحمه الله takes his name from his great grandfather, Ḥazm. It is well known that Ibn Ḥazm was born in Qurṭubah (Córdoba), however, some authors – such as Ibn Ḥajar[1] – refer to him as *al-Lablī* due to his ancestral home in Lablah (Niebla) in the Spanish province of Huelva, Andalusia. Ibn Ḥazm رحمه الله was born on the last day of Ramaḍān AH 384 which he had written himself and given to his student, Ṣāʿid b. Aḥmad, Abū al-Qāsim.

## Childhood and early life

Ibn Ḥazm رحمه الله spent all his life exclusively in al-Andalus except for a few months that he spent in al-Qayrawān in North Africa. He had intentions to

---

[1] Ibn Ḥajar, Aḥmad ibn ʿAlī, *Lisān al-mīzān* (Beirut: Dār al-Bashāʾir al-Islāmīyah, 2002), vol. 5, p. 489.

venture east to Baghdad and other centres of learning, however, this dream was never achieved. He was brought up in an affluent family since his father, who was also learned, served as a vizier to the Umayyad representative in al-Andalus until their fall from power. His father's vizierial position initially drew wealth and stability to the life of young Ibn Ḥazm, only to bring about various trials and tribulations later on.

Later in his life, Ibn Ḥazm الله رحمه also served the Umayyads as a vizier several times, but for short periods as these engagements concluded when they lost power. Due to the troubles and trials associated with his tenure, Ibn Ḥazm dedicated himself to learning the sacred Islamic sciences, writing, and teaching. He was famed for his deep and extensive knowledge and, as such, the Ẓāhirī *madhhab* spread all over al-Andalus. His critique and superior debating skills increased his fame during his lifetime. Moreover, he was known for his verbal altercations with the state-backed Mālikī *madhhab*, which occasionally invited his wrath.

While he was a skilled interlocutor, having mastered various sciences — including non-religious sciences, he was also a prolific writer and formidable debater. His mastery over argumentation and disputation on a whole array of genres made him a feared adversary.

By AH 399, the viceroys al-Manṣūr and al-Muẓaffar were displaced from power. As a result, Ibn Ḥazm's father was also discharged from his position and had to leave his palatine residence located in the outskirts of the austere city – al-Zāhirah. Ibn Ḥazm الله رحمه was about fifteen years old at the time. His family left their quarters, which were specifically for civil servants, and moved back to his childhood residence in Balāṭ Mughīth in eastern Qurṭubah (Córdoba).

These were troubling times for Ibn Ḥazm الله رحمه and his family; a life of peace and tranquility was soon followed by one of trials and persecution. During a period of civil unrest and turmoil, after successive changes in rulers, Ibn Ḥazm الله رحمه and his family faced oppression and tormenting tribulations which included imprisonment, exile, and oppressive official fines. Ibn Ḥazm's father, Aḥmad ibn Saʿīd, was imprisoned and all of his possessions were confiscated.

In addition to these dire times, the following years proved to be further sorrowful for Ibn Ḥazm ﷽; his elder brother Abū Bakr died from plague in AH 401 and, in the following year – AH 402 – at the age of just eighteen, he was grieved by the loss of his father. As if this was not enough, before he reached the age of twenty, he also faced the loss of his concubine whom he loved dearly; he mourned her for seven months.

In AH 403, the Berbers looted Qurṭubah (Córdoba); they burnt it, destroyed it, and slaughtered its inhabitants for two consecutive months. Ibn Ḥazm's family home in Balāṭ Mughīth was destroyed. Ibn Ḥazm, orphaned and vulnerable, was left with no option but to flee his birthplace. He entered al-Murīyah (Almería) in the beginning of AH 404.

Ibn Ḥazm ﷽ lived discreetly in al-Murīyah (Almería) seeking a life of peace; he learned and taught Islamic sciences while here. He also travelled to Mālaqah (Málaga) for a short while where he debated a Jewish scholar, which inspired him to write a book. The ruler of al-Murīyah (Almería) at the time, Khayrān, began questioning his motives and accused him of plotting a political insurgency. Consequently, Ibn Ḥazm ﷽ was sentenced to imprisonment for a few months and eventually exiled in AH 407. Thereafter, he sought refuge in the castle of Ḥiṣn al-Qaṣr (Aznalcázar), where he remained for a short while under the care of its king, Ibn Mughaffal.

Ibn Ḥazm ﷽ then traveled to Balansiyah (Valencia) and remained there for about two years. While there, al-Murtaḍī ʿAbd al-Raḥmān ibn Muḥammad, who was also in Balansiyah (Valencia), announced his succession to rule. Ibn Ḥazm was in favour of this announcement; his sympathy for the Umayyads drove him to join an expedition to regain Qurṭubah (Córdoba). However, they were defeated in Gharnāṭah (Granada) and Ibn Ḥazm was imprisoned by the Berbers.

After being released by the Berbers, Ibn Ḥazm ﷽ entered Qurṭubah (Córdoba) once again around AH 409 during the reign of Qāsim ibn Ḥamūd al-Mamūn, where he wrote his famous book, *Tawq al-Ḥamāmah (The Ring of the Dove)*. Around the year AH 414, Ibn Ḥazm got a brief relief from his troubles when the young ruler ʿAbd al-Raḥmān al-Mustaẓhir rose to power and appointed him as a vizier. However, this was only short-lived; lasting about seven weeks until the murder of al-Mustaẓhir. Ibn Ḥazm was, subsequently, imprisoned once more by the new ruler.

After brief vizierial stints, at around the age of thirty, Ibn Ḥazm رحمه الله became increasingly disillusioned with the return and sustained rule of the Umayyads. Nonetheless, he remained optimistic and, after a few years, he was reinstated as a vizier under the then viceroy. During such appointments, Ibn Ḥazm رحمه الله passionately dedicated himself to intellectual writing and learning, his pursuit of knowledge, as well as clarifying matters of the Dīn. He eventually concluded that he was created for other things; he left all vizierial and advisory positions and focused on the Sunnah and Āthār.

In AH 429, Ibn Ḥazm رحمه الله was imprisoned again by the Berbers. After his release, he travelled to different regions and got into religious disputations with various antagonists, which led to frequent imprisonments. When not in prison, Ibn Ḥazm was hiding from the authorities. After AH 430, at around the age of forty-five, Ibn Ḥazm entered Mayūraqah (Majorca) where he devoted most of his time to writing and composing his works. However, it was not long before he was in trouble with the authorities again.

In return for sanctuary in Mayūraqah (Majorca), Ibn Ḥazm رحمه الله was forced to issue legal edicts based on the Mālikī *madhhab* – not the Ẓāhirī – by Mayūraqah's (Majorca's) secretary, Abū al-ʿAbbās ibn Rashīq. Its inhabitants, like the inhabitants of al-Murīyah (Almería) previously, complained to their Qāḍīs, and Ibn Ḥazm was, yet again, faced with further trials and persecution. While here, he also had debates on theological issues with the foremost Ashʿarite of his era, Abū al-Walīd al-Bājī, who answered the antagonists' desperate calls for help after they failed to halt the intellectual juggernaut that was Ibn Ḥazm.

Around AH 440, at the age of about fifty-five, Ibn Ḥazm رحمه الله had to leave Mayūraqah (Majorca). He travelled to Dāniyah (Dénia), al-Murīyah (Almería), Ishbīl (Seville) and, finally, to his ancestral home.

Late in life, probably after AH 445, Ibn Ḥazm رحمه الله had to face another agonizing tragedy: the public burning of his books – demanded by al-Muʿtaḍid, the King of Ishbīl (Seville). Beaten by the trials, Ibn Ḥazm was eventually exiled to his ancestral home in Mūntaijā (Montija, in Huelva) on the order of al-Muʿtaḍid. In Mūntaijā (Montija), Ibn Ḥazm was able to resume writing and teaching; al-Muʿtaḍid had prevented him from doing so and threatened anyone who approached him for studies.

During this last period, Ibn Ḥazm رحمه الله focused on his writing and teaching the students who managed to study under him. Most of these students were young as the elder ones were well aware of the wrath and the promised punishment from the ruler. Some of his relatives may have also studied under him.

## His pursuit and quest for knowledge

One very well-known and oft-repeated account of how Ibn Ḥazm رحمه الله began seeking knowledge is that reported by his student Abū Muḥammad Ibn al-ʿArabī. The story goes that one day, when a friend of Ibn Ḥazm's father died, Ibn Ḥazm went for the funeral prayer at midday, entered the mosque, and sat down. One of his teachers signaled to him to pray the *taḥiyyat al-masjid*, which Ibn Ḥazm was unfamiliar with and the people said to him, "How can you not know about this prayer at your age?" Ibn Ḥazm was about 25–26 at the time of the alleged incident. An alternative account states that he was about to pray the *taḥiyyat al-masjid* after the ʿAsr prayer, when he was told to sit down.

Feeling humiliated and deeply ashamed, Ibn Ḥazm رحمه الله asked his teacher to direct him to the most learned jurist of the city: Abū ʿAbd Allāh ibn Daḥḥūn. Ibn Ḥazm read the *Muwaṭṭā'* of Imām Mālik to him as well as other books for approximately three years.

However, despite its popularity, this account is disputed and even rejected by some biographers. Many claims and explanations have been put forward to justify its lack of veracity – the main one being that Ibn Ḥazm رحمه الله was already studying with the local teachers in the grand mosque. Nonetheless, what is certain is that Ibn Ḥazm began seeking knowledge at the tender age of sixteen, around late AH 399 or early AH 400. He took up Ḥadīth studies with his teacher, Abū ʿUmar Aḥmad ibn Muḥammad al-Jasūr, and, thereby, became well-acquainted with the understanding of Ḥadīth.

## His teachers

Some of the numerous teachers who Ibn Ḥazm رحمه الله heard *ḥadīth* from and studied Islamic sciences under were Abū ʿUmar Aḥmad ibn Muḥammad al-Jasūr, as previously mentioned, Abū al-Qāsim ʿAbd al-Raḥmān ibn Abī Yazīd al-Miṣrī, Yaḥya ibn Masʿūd ibn Wajh al-Jannah, Qāḍī Yūnus ibn ʿAbd Allāh ibn Mughīth, Qāḍī Ḥumām ibn Aḥmad, Muḥammad ibn Saʿīd ibn Nabāt, ʿAbd Allāh ibn Rabīʿ al-Tamimī, ʿAbd al-Raḥmān ibn ʿAbd Allāh ibn Khālid, ʿAbd Allāh ibn Muḥammad ibn Uthmān, Abū ʿUmar Aḥmad ibn Muḥammad al-Ṭalamankī, ʿAbd Allāh ibn Yūsuf ibn Nāmī, and Abū ʿUmar ibn ʿAbd al-Barr al-Nimari. He also studied Fiqh under Abū ʿAbd Allāh ibn Daḥḥūn and ʿAlī ibn Saʿīd al-ʿAbdarī al-Mayurqī.

Moreover, Abū al-Khiyār Masʿūd ibn Sulaymān ibn Muflit was one of Ibn Ḥazm's رحمه الله famous and well-known teachers who taught him the various views of Fiqh and is also credited for instilling the inclination of the Ẓāhirī *madhhab* in him. Ibn Ḥazm studied Ḥadīth, Fiqh and other sciences from numerous other scholars who are too many to mention.

Ibn Ḥazm رحمه الله first studied the Mālikī *madhhab* in general under the clergy of Qurṭubah (Córdoba). Later, he studied the *madhab* in detail under Abū ʿAbd Allāh ibn Daḥḥūn for three years, after which he began to debate with the people. He then shifted his focus to the Shāfiʿī *madhhab* and eventually, the Ẓāhirī *madhhab*. In around AH 418–420, he began teaching the Ẓāhirī *madhhab* with his teacher – Abū al-Khiyār or Ibn Khiyār – in the grand mosque of Qurṭubah (Córdoba). The Mālikīs were infuriated; they lodged a complaint with the ruler who ordered a royal decree to ban them both from teaching.

It is no secret that Ibn Ḥazm رحمه الله championed the Ẓāhirī *madhhab;* he codified it, taught it, and spread it to unprecedented levels all over al-Andalus and the Maghreb. Ibn Ḥazm's view was simple: that only the Quran and authentic Sunnah had legislative authority and constituted evidence, and that all matters must be referred back to these two both generally and specifically when differences arose. He rejected views based on *qiyās* (analogy) and adhered to the general views and core evidences. He spent the remainder of his life defending and spreading the Ẓāhirī *madhhab* all over al-Andalus.

## His students

Ibn Ḥazm's رحمه الله students and those who narrated from him include Abū 'Abd Allāh al-Ḥumaydī, who greatly benefited from him. Abū 'Abd Allāh al-Ḥumaydī was an acclaimed historian who wrote *Jadhwat al-muqtabis fī tārīkh 'ulamā' al-andalus*. Another student, Ṣā'id ibn Aḥmad al-Andalusī, was also an established historian and geographer who authored the well-known *Ṭabaqāt al-Umam*. His son, Abū Rāfi' al-Faḍl, and a large group of people also benefitted from him. The last person to narrate from Ibn Ḥazm – who also had *ijāzah* from him – was Abū al-Ḥasan Shurayḥ ibn Muḥammad. Additionally, the likes of Abū Muḥammad ibn al-'Arabī – the father of the well-known Abū Bakr ibn al-'Arabi – studied all of his works with him for seven years with the exception of the last volume of his *Kitāb al-Fiṣal*.

## His works

Ibn Ḥazm's رحمه الله works were numerous; it is reported on numerous authorities that his son, Abū Rāfi' al-Faḍl, related that they reached around 400 volumes – a remarkable total of 80,000 pages. Undoubtedly, this deems him as the most prolific author in the history of Islam, (almost) on par with Ibn Jarīr al-Ṭabarī. His books varied in nature; most of them were his own compositions while others were his explanations of other works.

The public burning of Ibn Ḥazm's رحمه الله books was a tragedy. It was not executed by just a few isolated detractors or antagonists – nor even a group – but rather, it was state-backed. All of Ibn Ḥazm's books were burned. Inevitably, this event instilled fear in the people; his supporters who managed to get a hold of any of his books had no option but to conceal their existence in fear of reprisal. People were not only discouraged from reading Ibn Ḥazm's works, but even just looking at them was considered a tremendous risk. These adverse consequences, alongside the official ban that prevented Ibn Ḥazm from teaching, had deleterious effects on the works of Ibn Ḥazm. Thus, the outcome of this pure evil was the forever loss of these unfathomably precious gems that were the brilliant works of Ibn Ḥazm.

Nevertheless, from the heaps of their ashes and debris, remnants of his works were preserved through mentions or records from Ibn Ḥazm رحمه الله himself, his companions, or his students. There are records of the names of around 180 books, however, some scholars only consider 160 of them to be works authored by Ibn Ḥazm, and al-Dhahabī mentioned only seventy-four. Despite their small numbers, approximately forty works by Ibn Ḥazm have been published and remain intact till this day. This in itself is incredible; the recompilation of these almost-perished works epitomises the eminent virtue and stature of Ibn Ḥazm.

As listing all of the works of Ibn Ḥazm would be too lengthy, the following list is a brief mention of some of them.

1. *Al-iḥkām fī uṣūl al-aḥkām*
2. *Al-mujallā fī al-fiqh*
3. *Al-uṣūl wa al-furū‘*
4. *Qaṣīdah fī uṣūl al-fiqh al-ẓāhiriyyah*
5. *Risālah marātib al-‘ulūm*
6. *Jawāmi‘ al-sīrah*
7. *Kitāb al-fiṣal fī al-milal wa al-ahwā’ wa al-niḥal*
8. *Ibṭāl al-qiyās wa al-ra’y wa al-istiḥsān wa al-taqlīd wa al-ta‘līl*
9. *Kitāb al-akhlāq wa al-siyar fī mudāwāh al-nufūs* (the present work)
10. *Kitāb ḥajjat al-wadā’*
11. *Kitāb al-durrah fī mā yajibu i‘tiqāduhu* also known as *Risālah fī al-i‘tiqād*
12. *Marātib al-ijmā‘ fī al-‘ibādāt wa al-mu‘āmalāt wa al-i‘tiqādāt*
13. *Risālah ṭawq al-ḥamāmah fī al-ulfah wa al-ullāf*
14. *Asmā’ al-khulafā wa al-wulāh wa dhikr mudadihim*
15. *Asmā’ al-ṣaḥābah al-ruwāh wa mā li kulli wāḥid min al-aḥādīth*
16. *Risālah fī al-radd ‘alā Ibn al-Naghrīlah al-Yahūdī*
17. *Al-taqrīb li ḥadd al-manṭiq wa al-madkhal ilayhi bi al-alfāẓ al-‘āmiyyah wa al-amthilah al-fiqhiyyah*
18. *Jamharah ansāb al-‘arab*
19. *Al-risālah al-bāhirah fī al-radd ‘alā ahl al-aqwāl al-fāsidah*
20. *Al-muḥallā fī sharḥ al-mujallā bi al-ḥujaj wa al-āthār*

'Izz al-Dīn ibn 'Abd al-Salām said, "I have not seen any book on Islamic sciences greater than the likes of Ibn Ḥazm's *al-Muḥallá* and Shaykh Muwaffaq al-Dīn's *al-Mughnī*." Al-Dhahabī commented, "Shaykh 'Izz al-Dīn is right, and the third is al-Bayhaqī's *al-Sunan al-Kubrá*, and the fourth is Ibn 'Abd al-Barr's *al-Tamhīd*. Whoever obtains these volumes – if he is one of the intelligent *muftīs* and perseveres in reading them – is truly an *'ālim*."[2]

## His praise by the Ulamā'

Al-Ḥumaydī said, "I have not seen anyone like him; someone who had intelligence, an agile memory, generousness, and strong devotion to the Dīn all combined in him."[3]

He further praised and elevated the status of his teacher, Ibn Ḥazm, in more than just a few places in his book. One such example lies in the introduction, when he wrote, "These historical records and their respective science – I acquired most of them from my teacher, Ḥāfiẓ Abū Muḥammad 'Alī ibn Aḥmad ibn Ḥazm."[4]

Ibn Ḥajr also quoted al-Ḥumaydī to have said, "He was a *ḥāfiẓ* of Ḥadīth and its *fiqh* (understanding), able to [directly] deduce rulings from the Book (i.e. Quran) and Sunnah, an all-round expert in the various sciences, someone who acted upon his knowledge."[5]

Additionally, al-Dhahabī lauded Ibn Ḥazm with the following titles: *al-Imām, al-'Allāmah, al-Ḥāfiẓ, al-Faqīh, al-Mujtahid*[6] and "The Imam, the one and only, the ocean [of knowledge], the possessor of sciences and knowl-

---

[2] Al-Dhahabī, Shams al-Dīn Muḥammad ibn Aḥmad ibn 'Uthmān, *Siyar a'lām al-nubulā'* (Beirut: Mu'assasat al-Risālah, 1996), vol. 18, p. 193.

[3] Al-Ḥumaydī, Abū 'Abd Allah Muḥammad ibn Futūḥ ibn 'Abd Allāh, *Jadhwat al-muqtabis fī tārīkh 'ulamā' al-andalus* (Tunis: Dār al-Gharb al-Islāmī, 2008), 450.

[4] Al-Ḥumaydī, Abū 'Abd Allah Muḥammad ibn Futūḥ ibn 'Abd Allāh, *Jadhwat al-muqtabis fī tārīkh 'ulamā' al-andalus*, 55.

[5] Ibn Ḥajar, Aḥmad ibn 'Alī, *Lisān al-mīzān*, vol. 5, p. 490.

[6] Al-Dhahabī, Shams al-Dīn Muḥammad ibn Aḥmad ibn 'Uthmān, *Kitāb tadkirat al-ḥuffāẓ* (Beirut: Dār al-Kutub al-'Ilmīyah, 1955), vol. 3, p. 1146.

edge…"[7] and described him as follows: "He was extremely intelligent with a prolific memory such that his knowledge of the sciences was very extensive."[8] He also said, "He was an expert of the various sciences; he was devout, pious, ascetic, and eager for truth."[9]

Ibn Khallikān said of him, "He was humble, a possessor of many virtues and numerous works."[10]

Lastly, Shaykh al-Islām Ibn Taymiyyah said concerning Ibn Ḥazm رحمه الله, "He had faith, religious commitment, and a great deal of knowledge that no one can deny except one who is stubborn. The content of his books highlights his deep knowledge of different views and various circumstances, as well as his respect for the fundamentals of Islam and for the Messenger – an assembly of attributes which cannot be found in anyone else."[11]

## His family

Most biographers mention that Ibn Ḥazm رحمه الله had only one son, Abū Rāfiʻ al-Faḍl, who was also a scholar. However, some biographers mentioned that he also had other sons: Abū ʻUsāmah Yaʻqūb, Saʻīd, and Abū Sulaymān Muṣʻab, and a daughter. Nonetheless, such findings are skeptical and further research is required to confirm their veracity.

## His demise

The great polymath and phenomenon, Ibn Ḥazm رحمه الله, died on his estate in Mūntaijā (Montija), Munt Lishām, in his native ancestral home located in

---

[7] Al-Dhahabī, Shams al-Dīn Muḥammad ibn Aḥmad ibn ʻUthmān, *Siyar aʻlām al-nubulāʼ*, vol. 18, p. 184.

[8] Al-Dhahabī, Shams al-Dīn Muḥammad ibn Aḥmad ibn ʻUthmān, *Kitāb tadkirat al-ḥuffāẓ*, vols. 3, p. 1146.

[9] Al-Dhahabī, Shams al-Dīn Muḥammad ibn Aḥmad ibn ʻUthmān, *Kitāb tadkirat al-ḥuffāẓ*, vol. 3, p. 1146.

[10] Abū al-ʻAbbās Shams al-Dīn Aḥmad ibn Muḥammad ibn Abī Bakr ibn Khallikān, *Wafayāt al-aʻyān wa anbāʼ abnāʼ al-zamān* (Beirut: Dar Ṣādir, 1978), vol. 3, p. 325.

[11] Ibn Taymiyah, Aḥmad b. ʻAbd al-Ḥalīm, *Majmūʻ al-fatāwá* (Medina: King Fahd Glorious Qurʼan Printing Complex, 2004), vol. 4, pp. 19–20.

the west of al-Andalus, on 27/8 Shaʿbān in AH 456, at the age of seventy-one. Certainly, he left behind an everlasting legacy for the Muslim Ummah.

## Bibliography

Abū al-ʿAbbās Shams al-Dīn Aḥmad ibn Muḥammad ibn Abī Bakr ibn Khallikān. *Wafayāt al-aʿyān wa anbāʾ abnāʾ al-zamān.* 8 vols. Beirut: Dar Ṣādir, 1978.

Al-Dhahabī, Shams al-Dīn Muḥammad ibn Aḥmad ibn ʿUthmān. *Kitāb tadkirat al-ḥuffāẓ.* 4 vols. Beirut: Dār al-Kutub al-ʿIlmīyah, 1955.

———. *Siyar aʿlām al-nubulāʾ.* 29 vols. Beirut: Muʾassasat al-Risālah, 1996.

Al-Ḥumaydī, Abū ʿAbd Allah Muḥammad ibn Futūḥ ibn ʿAbd Allāh. *Jadhwat al-muqtabis fī tārīkh ʿulamāʾ al-andalus.* Tunis: Dār al-Gharb al-Islāmī, 2008.

Ibn Ḥajar, Aḥmad ibn ʿAlī. *Lisān al-mīzān.* 10 vols. Beirut: Dār al-Bashāʾir al-Islāmīyah, 2002.

Ibn Taymīyah, Aḥmad ibn ʿAbd al-Ḥalīm. *Majmūʿ al-fatāwá.* 37 vols. Medina: King Fahd Glorious Qurʾan Printing Complex, 2004.

# Contents

Chapter One

# *Introduction*

In the name of Allāh the Most Merciful and Clement: [O Allāh, I implore Your assistance. O Allāh, bless Muḥammad and his family and grant them peace]. Abū Muḥammad ʿAlī ibn Aḥmad ibn Saʿīd ibn Ḥazm al-Andalusī رضي الله عنه has said:

1 Praise be to Allāh for His great gifts. May Allāh bless [our master] Muḥammad, His servant, the seal of His Prophets and Messengers; may He grant them eternal blessings. I rely on Him for any ability and strength I may have, and I seek His aid and protection against all the various terrors and ills of this world. And may He deliver me from all horror and suffering in the next world.

2 Now, I have gathered together in this book numerous ideas which Allāh, the provider of intellect, has enabled me to profit from as day succeeded day, [and year succeeded year] and circumstances altered, permitting me to understand the vicissitudes[1] of fate and to control its fluctuations, to the extent that I have devoted the larger part of my life to it. I have chosen to master these problems by study and contemplation, rather than throw myself into the various sensual pleasures which attract most souls on this earth, and rather than amass unnecessary wealth. I have gathered together all my observations into this book in the hope that the Almighty may allow it to benefit whichever of His servants He wishes who has access to [is capable of understanding] my book, in the matters over which I have slaved, devoting

---

[1] *vicissitude*: The fact of change or mutation taking place in a particular thing or within a certain sphere; the uncertain changing or mutability of something.

all my efforts to them, and reflecting at length upon them. I hope that it will be well received, and I present it with good intentions and blessings [with a good heart].

---

This book will benefit a person more than financial treasures and possessions of property, if he meditates upon it, and if Allāh enables him to make good use of it. As for myself, my hope in this enterprise is to win the greatest reward from Allāh, since my intention is to help His servants, to remedy whatever is corrupt in their character, and to heal the sickness of their souls. I beseech the assistance of Allāh [Almighty, we wish only for Allāh, the best of defenders].

Chapter Two

# *Treatment of the Souls*

3    The pleasure which a prudent man has from his own good sense, a scholar from his knowledge, a wise man from his wisdom, the pleasure of anyone who works hard in ways pleasing to Almighty Allāh, is greater than the pleasure which the gourmet[1] has from his food, a drinking man from his tipple,[2] a lover from the act of love, a conqueror from his conquest, a reveller from his amusements [the player from his game] or a commander from giving orders. The proof of this is that the wise man, the prudent man, the scholar, the practising Muslim, and all those that we have mentioned are capable of enjoying these pleasures as much as the man who indulges in them. They have the same feelings and desires as those who hasten to satisfy them. But they have deliberately refrained and turned away from them, preferring to seek after moral excellence. None can judge these two [kinds of pleasure] except someone who has known both; not someone who has known one and not the other.

4    [As things happen one after the other] If you look deeply into worldly matters you will become melancholy[3] and will end by reflecting upon the ephemeral nature of everything here below, and the fact that truth lies only in striving for the hereafter, since every ambition to which you might cling will end in tears: either the goal is snatched from you, or you have to give the attempt up before you reach it. One of these two endings is inevitable except in the

---

[1]    *gourmet*: A connoisseur in the delicacies of the table.
[2]    *tipple*: Drink, liquor for drinking; especially strong drink.
[3]    *melancholy*: Sadness and depression of spirits; a condition of gloom or dejection, especially when habitual or constitutional.

search for Allāh Almighty and Powerful. Then the result is always joy, both immediate and eternal. The immediate joy is because you stop worrying about the things which usually worry people; this leads to an increase in the respect paid to you by friends and enemies alike. The eternal joy is that of Paradise.

5 I have tried to find one goal which everyone would agree to be excellent and worthy of being striven after. I have found one only: to be free from anxiety. When I reflected upon it, I realized that not only do all agree in valuing it and desiring it, but I also perceived that, despite their many different passions and aspirations and preoccupations and desires, they never make the slightest gesture unless it is designed to drive anxiety far away. One man loses his way, another comes close to going wrong, finally another is successful—but he is a rare man, and success is rare, [O, All-knowing Allāh]. Dispelling anxiety is a goal upon which all nations agree from the time when the Almighty created the world until the day when this world will pass away and be followed by the Day of Judgment—and their actions are directed to this goal alone. In the case of every other objective there will always be some people who do not desire it.

For example, some people are not religious and do not take eternity into account. There are some who by nature and inclination prefer obscurity to fame [the obscurity of satisfied passion]. There are some who have no interest in amassing a fortune, preferring abstinence to ownership; this was the case with many of the Prophets عليهم السلام and those who followed their example, ascetics, and philosophers. There are some who by nature dislike sensual pleasures and scorn those who seek after them, such as those men we have just mentioned, and who prefer to lose a fortune rather than gain one. Some prefer ignorance to knowledge, in fact most of the people that you see in the street are like this. These are the objectives of people who have no other aim in life. Nobody in the whole world, from the time of its creation until its end, would deliberately choose anxiety, and would not desire to drive it far away.

6 When I had arrived at this great piece of wisdom, when I had discovered

this amazing secret, when Allāh Almighty had opened the eyes of my mind [spirit] to see this great pleasure, I began to search for the way which would truly enable me to dispel anxiety, that precious goal desired by every kind of person, whether ignorant or scholarly, good or evil. I found it in one place alone, in the action of turning towards Allāh, the Almighty and Powerful, in pious works performed with an eye to eternity.

7 Thus the only reason that someone chases after riches is to dispel the anguish of poverty. The only reason that someone seeks fame is to dispel the anxiety of seeing someone else outdo him. The only reason that someone chases after pleasures is to dispel the anxiety of missing them. The only reason someone chases after knowledge is to dispel the anxiety of being ignorant about something. People enjoy listening to other peoples' conversations and gossip only because it dispels the anxiety of being alone and isolated. People eat, drink, make love, wear clothes, play games, build a shelter, mount a horse, and go for walks, only in order to avoid the reverse of all these actions and every other kind of anxiety.

8 In all the actions listed here, anyone who pauses to reflect will see that anxieties inevitably occur, such as problems which arise in the course of the action, the impossibility of performing the impossible, the fleeting nature of any achievements, and the inability to enjoy something because of some difficulty. There are also bad consequences which arise from every success: fear of one's rival, attacks by the jealous, theft by the covetous, loss to an enemy, not to mention criticism, sin, and other such things. On the other hand, I have found that actions performed with an eye on eternity are free from *every kind* of fault, free from *every stain*, and a true means of dispelling anxiety. I have found that the man who is striving for eternity may be sorely tested by bad fortune on his way but does not worry; on the contrary, he is glad, because the trial to which he is subjected gives rise to hope, which aids him in his endeavour and sets him more firmly on the path towards his true desire. I have found that when he finds his way blocked by an obstacle, he does not worry, because it is not his fault, and he did not choose the actions that he will have to answer for. I have seen such a man be glad, when others have wished evil upon him, and be glad when he has undergone some trial,

and be glad, always [living] in a permanent state of joy while others are permanently the opposite. You should therefore understand that there is only one objective to strive for, it is to dispel anxiety; and only one path leads to this, and that is the service of the Most High, Allāh. Everything else is misguided and absurd.

9 Do not use your energy except for a cause more noble than yourself. Such a cause cannot be found except in Almighty Allāh Himself: to preach the truth, to defend womanhood, to repel humiliation which your Creator has not imposed upon you, and to help the oppressed. Anyone who uses his energy for the sake of the vanities of the world is like someone who exchanges gemstones for gravel.

10 There is no nobility in anyone who lacks faith.

11 The wise man knows that the only fitting price for his soul is a place in Paradise.

12 Shayṭān sets his traps under the cover of finding fault with hypocrisy. It can happen that someone refrains from doing a good deed for fear of being thought a hypocrite. [If Shayṭān whispers such an idea in your ear, take no notice; that will frustrate him.]

Chapter Three

# *The Mind and Repose*

Do not listen to what other people say. Listen only to the Words of the Creator. That is the way to a completely sound mind and to perfect repose.[1]

13 Anyone who believes himself safe from all criticism and reproach is out of his mind.

14 Anyone who studies deeply and disciplines his soul not to rest until it has found the truth, even if it is painful at first, will take more pleasure in criticism than in praise. Indeed, if he hears people praise him, even if it is well-deserved, he will become proud, and his virtue will be corrupted.

If he hears people praise him and the praise is undeserved, he will be pleased, but wrongly so, and this is a serious fault. On the other hand, if he hears people criticise him and it is deserved, he might be led to correct the behaviour that led to it. This criticism would be a piece of considerable good luck that only a fool would ignore. If someone is criticised unjustly and he controls himself, he will gain merit by his meekness[2] and patience. Furthermore, all the good works ever done by his critic will be credited to him, and he will gain the benefit of them on Judgment Day when they will stand him in very good stead[3] when he needs them, although they were not a result of his own efforts. And this is a supreme piece of good luck which would be mad to disdain. If he does not hear people's praise, what they say or do

---

[1] *repose*: Relief or respite from exertion, toil, trouble, or excitement.
[2] *meekness*: The quality of being meek; gentleness of spirit; humility.
[3] *in good (etc.) stead*: in good (etc.) circumstances.

not say makes no difference to him. But it is a different matter with their criticism, he wins either way, whether he hears their criticism or not.

15 If it were not for the words of the Prophet ﷺ about "good praise"[4] which "brings to the believers the express good news of the happiness which has been promised," it might have been a sign of wisdom to prefer being criticized – even unjustly – to being praised with good reason. But these words were spoken. The promised happiness "will always arise from merit, not from absence of merit; it will reward only the object of praise, not merely the fact that praises were uttered."

16 There is no difference between virtues and vices, between acts of devotion and acts of rebellion, except in as far as the soul feels attracted or repelled. Happy the man whose soul finds pleasure in virtue and good deeds, fleeing vice and rebellion. And unhappy the man whose soul finds pleasure in vice and rebellion, fleeing virtue and good deeds. This is nothing less than the sacred order of things ordained by the providence of the Almighty, Allāh.

17 Anyone who strives after eternity is on the side of the Angels. Anyone who strives after evil is on the side of the demons. Anyone who seeks fame and victory is on the side of the tigers. Anyone who seeks sensual pleasures is on the side of the [dumb] beasts. Anyone who seeks money for its own sake, not for spending on pious obligations and praiseworthy acts of charity, is too base, too vile to be compared with a beast. He resembles rather the waters which gather in caves in inaccessible places: no animal profits at all from them, [except now and then a bird; then the wind and the sun dry up what is left. And the same thing happens to possessions which are not consecrated to pious works].

18 A wise man has no satisfaction in a quality which sets him below tigers, dumb beasts, and inanimate objects. He rejoices only in his progress in that virtue

---

4 ❂ This is in reference to the *ḥadīth* of Abū Dhar رضي الله عنه who said that the Messenger of Allah ﷺ was asked, "Tell us about a person who does some good deed and people praise him, will this be considered as showing off?" He ﷺ replied, "This is the glad tidings which a believer receives (in this life)." (Translation from `https://sunnah.com`)

by which Allāh distinguishes him from these same tigers, dumb beasts, and inanimate objects: this is the virtue of intelligence which he shares with the Angels.

19 Anyone who feels proud of courage which is not applied in its normal direction, i.e. the service of Almighty Allāh, let him understand that the tiger is braver than him, that the lion, the wolf, and the elephant are braver than him.

20 Anyone who glories in his own physical strength, let it be known to him that the mule, the ox, and the elephant are physically stronger than him.

21 Anyone who glories is his ability to carry heavy weights, let it be known to him that the donkey can carry greater weights.

22 Anyone who glories in his ability to run, let it be known to him that the dog and the hare run faster than him.

23 Anyone who glories in the sound of his voice, let it be known to him that many of the birds have sweeter voices than him, and the sound of the flutes is more exquisite and charming than the sound of his voice. How can anyone take pride or satisfaction in qualities in which these animals are superior?

24 But a man whose intellect is strong, whose knowledge is extensive, and whose deeds are good, should rejoice because only the Angels and the best of men are superior to him in these matters.

25 Allāh says, ﴿وَأَمَّا مَنْ خَافَ مَقَامَ رَبِّهِۦ وَنَهَى ٱلنَّفْسَ عَنِ ٱلْهَوَىٰ ۝ فَإِنَّ ٱلْجَنَّةَ هِىَ ٱلْمَأْوَىٰ ۝﴾ «Anyone who fears the majesty of Allāh, and controls himself against passion, he shall have Paradise for his refuge.» (Quran 79:40–41) These words encapsulate all virtue: *to control oneself against passion* means in fact to turn away from one's natural tendency towards anger and lust, things which are both under the dictates of passion. Then all that is left for the soul to use is the intellect which Allāh has given it, the good sense which distinguishes it from the beasts, from insects or vermin, and from tigers.

26 "Never lose your temper,"[5] as Allāh's Prophet ﷺ said to a man asking his advice, and[6] his ﷺ command that a person love for others what he loves for himself[7] together encapsulate the whole of virtue. Indeed, the fact that the Prophet forbade all anger implies that although the soul has been given the ability to be angry, it should refrain from this passion, and the [Prophet's] commandment *to do as you would be done by* implies that the souls should turn away from the strong force of greed and lust and uphold the authority or the means of justice which springs from rationality which is part of a reasonable soul.

27 I have seen the majority of people—except those who Allāh Almighty has protected, and they are few—throw themselves into the miseries, the worries, and fatigues of this world, and pile up a mountain of sin which will mean that they enter hellfire in the Hereafter and will have no advantage from the perfidious[8] intentions which they nurse so carefully, such as wishing for an inflation of prices which would bring disaster upon the children, the innocent, or wishing the worst trials upon those they hate. They know very well that these bad intentions will not necessarily bring about what they desire or guarantee its advent, and if they clarified and improved their intentions they would hasten the repose of their spirits. They would then have the time to devote themselves to their own business and would thus profit a great deal in addition to the return of their souls to Allāh, and all this without having

---

5 ✦ This is in reference to the *ḥadīth* collected by Imam al-Bukhārī رحمه الله. Abū Hurayrah رضي الله عنه reported that a man said to the Prophet ﷺ, "Advise me!" The Prophet ﷺ replied, "Do not become angry." The man asked (the same) again and again, and the Prophet ﷺ said every time, "Do not become angry." The original Arabic is لَا تَغْضَبْ which can also be translated as "Don't lose your temper."

6 ✦ The second part of this sentence was originally translated as ‹...and as he ﷺ also said commanding him, "Do as you would be done by,"› This might have been due to misreading the word أمره which can be read both as أَمَرَهُ and أُمِرَهُ. The latter seems to be what is intended since that is how it occurs in Source B and there is no evidence to suggest that the persons mentioned in the two narrations are one and the same. Allāh knows best.

7 ✦ This is in reference to the *ḥadīth* collected by Imam al-Bukhārī رحمه الله. Anas ibn Mālik رضي الله عنه reported that the Prophet ﷺ said, "None of you [truly] believes until he loves for his brother what he loves for himself."

8 *perfidious*: ...deliberately faithless; basely treacherous.

at all hastened or delayed the realization of their desires. Is there any worse deception than the attitude which we warn against here, and is there any greater happiness than the one which we are promoting?

28  When we contemplate the duration of this Universe, we see it limited to the present moment, which is nothing but the point which separates two infinities of time. The past and the future are as meaningless as if they did not exist. Is anyone more misguided than the man who barters an eternal future for a moment which passes quicker than the blink of an eye?

29  When a man is asleep, he leaves the world and forgets all joy and all sorrow. If he kept his spirit in the same state on waking, he would know perfect happiness.

30  A man who harms his family and his neighbors is viler than them. Anyone who returns evil for evil is as bad as them. Anyone who refrains from returning evil is their master, their superior, and the most virtuous among them.

Chapter Four

# *Knowledge*

31  If knowledge had no other merit than to make the ignorant fear and respect you, and the scholars love and honour you, this would be good enough reason to seek after it. Let alone all its other merits in this world and the next!

32  If ignorance had no other fault than to make the ignorant man jealous of knowledgeable men and jubilant at seeing more people like himself, this by itself would be a reason enough to oblige us to flee it. Let alone the other bad results of this evil in this world and the next!

33  If knowledge and the action of devoting oneself to it had no purpose except to free the man who seeks it from the exhausting anxieties and many worries which afflict the mind, that alone would certainly be enough to drive us to seek knowledge. But what should we say of the other benefits too numerous to list, the least of which are the above-mentioned, and all of which accrue to the knowledgeable man. In search of benefits as small as these, the petty kings have worn themselves out in seeking distraction from their anxieties in games of chess, dicing, wine, song, hunting expeditions, and other pastimes which bring nothing but harm in this world and the next and absolutely no benefit.

34  If the scholar who has spent long peaceful hours [at his studies] stopped to think how his knowledge has protected him against humiliation at the hands of the ignorant, and against anxiety about unknown truths, and what joy it has brought him by enabling him to solve problems which others find insoluble, he would certainly increase his expressions of gratitude to Allāh

and rejoice more in the knowledge that he has and desire even more to add to it.

35 Anyone who spends his time studying something inferior, abandoning higher studies of which he is capable, is like someone who sows corn in a field capable of growing wheat, or who plants bushes in soil which could support palm trees and olives.

36 To spread knowledge among those incapable of understanding it would be as harmful as giving honey and sugary confections to someone with a fever, or giving musk and amber to someone with a migraine caused by an excess of bile.

37 A man who is a miser with his knowledge is worse than a man who is a miser with his money, for the latter is afraid of using up what he possesses but the former is being mean with something which does not get used up and is not lost when it is given away.

38 Anyone who has a natural inclination towards a branch of knowledge, even if it is inferior to other branches, should not abandon it, or he would be like someone who plants coconuts in al-Andalus or olive trees in India where neither would produce fruit.

39 The most noble branches of knowledge are those which bring you close to the Creator and help you to be pleasing to Him.

40 When you compare yourself with others in matters of wealth, position, and health, you should look at people less favoured than yourself.[1] When you compare yourself with others in matters of religion, knowledge, and virtue, look at people who are better than yourself.

---

[1] ☼ This is in reference to the *ḥadīth* collected by Imam al-Bukhārī and Imam Muslim. Abū Hurayrah رضي الله عنه reported that the Prophet said, "Look at those who are below you, and do not look at those who are above you, for that is more likely to hold you back from belittling the blessings that Allāh has bestowed upon you."

41   The mysterious branches of knowledge are like a strong drug which benefits a strong body but damages a weak one. In the same way, the esoteric[2] branches of knowledge enrich a strong mind, and refine it, purifying it of its flaws, but destroy a weak mind.

42   If a madman threw himself as deeply into good sense as he throws himself as deeply into madness, he would surely be wiser than al-Ḥasan al-Baṣrī,[3] Plato of Athens,[4] and Vuzurgmihr the Persian.[5]

43   Intelligence has its limits; it is useless unless it is based upon the guidance of religion or on good fortune in this world.

44   Do not harm your soul by experimenting with corrupt views in order to demonstrate their corruption to someone who has consulted you, otherwise you will lose your soul. If you shield yourself from acting in a detestable way, any criticism that can be thrown at you by a man of corrupt beliefs because you disagree with him is better than his respect and better than the bad effect on both of you if you committed these detestable acts.

45   Guard against taking pleasure in any way that will harm your soul and is not required of you by the religious law nor by virtue.

---

2   *esoteric*: Of philosophical doctrines, treatises, modes of speech, etc.: Designed for, or appropriate to, an inner circle of advanced or privileged disciples; communicated to, or intelligible by, the initiated exclusively. Hence of disciples: Belonging to the inner circle, admitted to the esoteric teaching. Opposed to exoteric.

3   Al-Ḥasan al-Baṣrī (d. AH 100 / 718 CE) was a great Muslim traditionalist and Ṣūfī ascetic. In the history of Islām he looms large for his literary writings and moral sayings. See Ibn Khallikān, *Wafayāt* (Cairo: Bulaq, n.d.) vol. I, p. 227. He was born and lived in Basra, southern Iraq.

4   Plato, the famous Greek philosopher, d. 347 BC, disciple of Socrates, visited Egypt and lived there for one year and learned before Egyptian wise men in 'Ayn Shams. Jamāl al-Dīn Abū al-Ḥasan al-Qafṭī, *Tārikh al-Ḥukamā'*, edited by Julius Lippert (Leipzig, 1903) p. 16, also Abū Sulaymān al-Manṭiqī al-Sijistānī, *Ṣiwān al-Ḥikmah wa Thalāth Rasā'il*, edited by A. Badawī, (Tehran, 1974) p. 84, 128ff.

5   Vuzurgmihr was the minister of the ancient Persian king, Khusrau Nushirwan, and his son's tutor. He is famous for his wise sayings, which are often quoted in Arabic sources, and he is said to have been the first to translate the Indian text *Kalila wa Dimna* into the Persian language.

46 Knowledge no longer exists if one has ignored the attributes of the Almighty Great Creator.

47 There is no worse calamity for knowledge and for scholars than when outsiders intrude. They are ignorant and think they are knowledgeable; they ruin everything and believe that they are helping.

48 Anyone who is seeking happiness in the Hereafter, wisdom in this world, the best way to behave, the sum of all moral qualities, and the practice of all virtues, should take as his model Muḥammad, the Prophet of Allāh and emulate as far as possible the Prophet's morals and behaviour. May Allāh help us to take him as an example, by His grace, amīn [amīn]!

49 The ignorant have annoyed me on two occasions in my lifetime. First, when they spoke of things they did not know, at a time when I was equally ignorant; the second time when they kept silent in my presence [in the days when I had learnt something]. In the same way they were always silent about matters which would have benefited them to speak about, and spoke about matters which brought them no benefit.

50 Scholars have brought me pleasure on two occasions in my lifetime: first, they taught me when I was ignorant; the second time was when they conversed with me after I had been taught.

51 One of the merits of religious knowledge and asceticism in this world is that Almighty Allāh does not put it within the reach of anyone except those who are worthy of it and deserve it. One of the disadvantages of the great things of this world, wealth and fame, is that they are mostly given to people who are unworthy of them and do not deserve them.

52 Anyone who is seeking after virtue should keep company with the virtuous and should take no companion with him on his way except the noblest friend, one of those people who is sympathetic, charitable, truthful, sociable, patient, trustworthy, loyal, magnanimous, pure in conscience, and a true friend.

53  Anyone who is seeking fame, fortune, and pleasure will keep company only with those people who resemble mad dogs and sly foxes: they will take for their travelling companions only people [inimical[6] to his belief] who are cunning and depraved in nature.

54  The usefulness of the knowledge [of good] in the practice of virtue is considerable: anyone who knows the beauty of virtue will practise it, though it may be rarely. Knowing the ugliness of vice, he will avoid it, though it may be rarely. The man with knowledge of good will listen to soundly-based praise and desire it for himself. He will listen to talk of evil and desire to avoid it. From this premise it necessarily follows that knowledge has a part in every virtue, and ignorance has a part in every vice. A man who has had no instruction in the knowledge [of good] will not practise virtue unless he has an extremely pure nature, a virtuous constitution. It is the particular state of the Prophets عليهم السلام for Allāh has taught them virtue in its entirety, without them having learnt it from men.

55  It is true that I have seen among the common people some who, by their excellent behaviour and morals, were not surpassed by any wise man, any scholarly, self-controlled man. But this is very rare. And I have seen men who have studied the different branches of knowledge, who have a good knowledge of the messages of the Prophets    and the advice of the philosophers and who nevertheless surpass the most wicked in their bad behaviour, their depravity, both internal and external. These are the worst of all creatures. This is very common and I therefore perceive that these two [moral attitudes] are a favour which is granted or withheld by Allāh Almighty.

---

[6]  *inimical*: Adverse or injurious in tendency or influence; harmful, hurtful.

Chapter Five

# *Morals and Behaviour*

56  Take care to have a reputation of being a man of good intention. Beware of gaining a reputation of being devious or people will avoid you more and more and you will finish by being harmed or even lost.

57  Train yourself to think about the things that frighten you. If they come to pass, you will not be so worried by them. You will not lose anything by growing accustomed to the thought of them, and your pleasure will be greater or even doubled if something nice or unexpected happens.

58  When worries multiply, they will all fall to the ground [A way out will be found].

59  A deceitful man may occasionally keep his word to a lucky man, and a faithful man may occasionally betray an unlucky man. Happy is he who in this world is not obliged by fate to put his friends to the test.

60  Do not worry about a man who wishes you ill. If fortune favours you, he is lost and your luck will protect you. If fortune does not favour you, then anyone can harm you.

61  Blessed is the man who knows his own faults better than others know them.

62  Patience in the face of others' insolence is of three kinds: patience with someone who has power over you when you have none over him; patience with someone you have power over when he has none over you; finally patience with someone when neither of you has power over the other. The first kind is humiliating and degrading; it is not a virtue. The advice for someone who

is afraid of such an intolerable situation would be to abandon everything and run away. The second kind is a virtue, it is charitable, it is true meekness[1] which characterizes virtuous souls. The third sort consists of two kinds. The insolence may arise from a misunderstanding or from fear, and the one at fault may realize the ugliness of his act and regret it. To be patient with him would be a virtue and an obligation; this is true magnanimity.[2] But with a person who overestimates his own value and is proud and arrogant and feels no regret for his action, to tolerate this is humiliating, it encourages the wrongdoer in his wrongdoing, because he will act even more violently and it would be stupid to respond in the same way. The wisest course of action is to let him know that you could fight back but that you are refraining from doing so because he is beneath contempt and unworthy of your attention. No more is necessary. As for the insolent behaviour of the lower classes, the only remedy is to punish it.

63 Anyone who mingles with the crowd is never short of worries to pain him, or sins to regret on the day when he will return to Allāh, or anger to give him a pain in the liver [heart],[3] or humiliation to make him hang his head. Then what shall I say about someone who is intimate with people and always in their company? Solitude is where you will find dignity, repose, happiness,

---

[1] *meekness*: The quality of being meek; gentleness of spirit; humility.

[2] *magnanimity*: Nobility of feeling; superiority to petty resentment or jealousy; generous disregard of injuries.

[3] Ibn Ḥazm's رحمه الله text states clearly that he has been told that the spleen is the seat of both good and bad temper. He may have had this idea from reading the works of Ibn Qutaybah (d. AH 276 / 889 CE), who reported it from Wahb ibn Munabbih, who in turn ascribed it to the Torah. Allāh created man from the four elements water, earth, fire, and air; wet, dry, hot, and cold. Allāh then gave him a mind in his head, covetousness in his kidneys, anger is his liver, determination in his heart, fear and terror in his lungs, emotions, laughter, and tears in his spleen, his happiness and sadness in his face, and in the human body he made 360 joints. This is a medical matter which may be true but it is for doctors to say. See vol. 2, p. 62 of *'Uyūn al-Akhbār* (Cairo: al-Mu'assasah al-Miṣrīyyah al-'Ammāh li-Ta'līf, n.d.).

⟡ During the Battle of Ṣiffīn, 'Iyāḍ ibn Khalīfah heard 'Alī رضي الله عنه say, "Indeed, the intellect is in the heart, mercy in the liver, compassion in the spleen, and the soul in the lungs." (Reported by al-Bukhārī in *al-Adab al-Mufrad*, ḥadīth no. 547. Shaykh al-Albānī declared it *ḥasan*. See the recension of *al-Adab al-Mufrad* by Muḥammad Fu'ād 'Abd al-Bāqī. [Beirut: Dār al-Bashā'ir al-Islāmīyyah, 1989]).

and security. You should treat company like a fire. Warm yourself but do not fall in; ["You may draw near but without going right in"].

64  If the company of the people had only the two following faults, it would be enough to keep us away: the first is letting out vital secrets during a friendly meeting, secrets which otherwise would never have been revealed. The second is showing off, putting our immortality[4] in mortal peril. There is no other escape from these two trials than to withdraw into absolute solitude, far from people altogether.

65  Do not put off to tomorrow what you can do today. If you recognize this obligation you will make haste to do today even very small preparations for tomorrow, for if a small number of tasks are left to mount up they become a great number. In fact they have become too many to do and the whole enterprise will be wrecked.

66  Do not despise any of the actions that you hope to see counted in your favour on the Day of Resurrection. By doing them now, even in small measure, these actions will eventually outweigh the number of your sins which would otherwise add up to sufficient reason to throw you into hellfire.

67  With depression, poverty, misfortune, and fear, the pain is only felt by the sufferer. People looking at them from the outside have no idea what they are like. On the other hand, with false judgment, shame, and sin, only the onlooker sees how horrible they are! The person who is sunk deep in them does not perceive this.

68  Security, health, and wealth are only appreciated by a person who does not have them. Anyone who has them does not appreciate them. On the other hand, a sound judgment and virtue and working towards eternity, their value is known only to those who share in them. Anyone who has no share in them has no knowledge of what they are like.

---

4  *immortality*: The condition of being celebrated through all time; enduring fame or remembrance.

69 The first person to break away from a deceiver is the one whom the deceiver had deceived. The first person to detest a false witness is the person whom the false witness had wrongly supported with his testimony. The first person to despise an adulterous woman is the man who caused her to commit adultery.

70 As far as we know, nothing can be degraded and then resume its natural state without great trouble and difficulty. What can we say about the man whose head is poisoned by intoxication every night? Indeed, a mind which drives its master towards its own deprivation every night must be a mind condemned.

71 The highway [or a long journey] is fatiguing, a quiet retreat is restorative. Too much wealth makes for greed. A small fortune makes for contentment.

72 The plans of an intelligent man may go wrong. The plans of a stupid man never go right.

73 Nothing is more harmful to a governor than to be surrounded by a great number of unemployed people. A prudent ruler knows how to keep them busy without being unfair to them, otherwise they will overwhelm him with petty matters.

Anyone who invites his enemies to come closer to him is suicidal.[5]

74 Anyone who sees an important person too often regards him as less eminent and less important.

75 Parading, putting on, for example, a severe and discontented air, this is the veil with which ignorant people who have risen in the world try to cover their ignorance.

76 A wise man should not delude himself about friendship which started when he was in power, because everyone was his friend then.

---

[5]  ✿ This appears as a separate point in Source D.

77 The best person to help you in your affairs is someone with equal interest in their success. Do not get anyone to help you who would be just as well off elsewhere.

78 Do not respond to talk which is brought by someone on the part of a third person, unless you are sure that the latter did say it, because the one who brought lies to you will go away carrying the truth [the unpleasant truth which you will have told him and which he will hawk around].

79 Put your trust in a pious man, even if the religion that he practises is a different one from your own. Do not put your trust in anyone who scorns sacred things, even if he claims to belong to your own religion. As for a man who defies the commandments of the Almighty, do not ever trust him with anything you care greatly about.

80 I have noticed that people are more generous with their opinions than with their pennies. In my long study of this matter, this has never been disproved despite countless observations. Since I cannot understand the cause of this, I suppose it must be innate in human nature.

81 It is the height of injustice to deny a habitual wrongdoer the opportunity of doing an occasional good deed.

82 When you get rid of one enemy you see a great many others advancing.

83 I have never seen anything more lifelike than the shadow-theatre with its little actors mounted on wooden handles that are turned rapidly so that some disappear and others appear.[6]

84 For a long time I have been thinking about death. I had certain dear friends, as closely bound to me by the bonds of sincere affection as the soul is bound to the body. After they died, some of them appeared to me in dreams. Others did not. While one of the latter was alive, we had each promised to visit the

---

[6] This is an important historical reference to shadow-theatres in al-Andalus in the time of Ibn Ḥazm. c.f. Ibn Ḥazm, *al-Fiṣal*, vol. 1, p. 110 and vol. 5, p. 6.

other in a dream after we had died, if at all possible. But I have not seen him at all since he preceded me into the other world. I do not know whether he has forgotten or been engaged.

85 The oblivion of the soul who forgets the state it was in in the world of temptation [its first abode] while waiting for the resurrection of the body [to enter the body] is like the oblivion of someone who has fallen into mud and has sunk [all his promises] together with everything which he knew before and which was familiar to him. I have also reflected for a long time about this matter, and it seems to be that there is another possible explanation in addition to the one just mentioned. I have studied a sleeping person at the moment when his soul leaves his body, and his senses sharpen to the point of being able to see the unseen; the soul forgets completely, absolutely, the state which it was in just a moment before falling asleep, although it was so recent.

The soul knows other states in which it is endowed with memory and feelings, it can be pleased, it can be hurt. The joys of sleep are felt even during the sleep, for the sleeper feels happy, he dreams, he is afraid, he is sad, even in his sleep.

86 The soul is not happy except in the company of a soul. The body is heavy and wearying. This is proved by the haste with which one buries the body of a loved one when the soul has departed from it, and by the sorrow caused by the disappearance of the soul although the corpse is still there.

87 I have never seen Shayṭān use a worser trick, or an uglier or a more foolish one, than when he puts two phrases onto the tongues of those who follow him. The first is when someone excuses his own evil deed by alleging that someone has done the same to him. The second is when someone makes light of doing evil today because he did evil yesterday, or he does wrong in one sense because he has already done it in another. These two phrases excuse and facilitate evil-doing; they bring it into the arena of what is acceptable, tolerable, and not to be criticized.

88 Be mistrustful if you are able to be sufficiently careful and cautious, but if you cannot check on them, you will have to trust people. This will bring you peace of mind.

89 The definition of generosity, the supreme objective of generosity, is to give away the entire surplus of your possessions in charitable works. The best charitable work is to bring relief to a neighbour in need, a poor relative, and a man who has lost his own possessions and is close to ruin. Anyone who holds on to this superfluous money without spending it in one of these ways is an example of miserliness. And he should be praised and criticized in proportion to whether he is more or less generous in this way. Anything given to causes which are not these charitable ones is squandered, and the action is blameworthy. It is virtuous to give to someone in greater need part of what you need to keep alive; this is a nobler act of self sacrifice than plain generosity is. To keep what you need is neither praiseworthy nor blameworthy but simply fair. To carry out one's obligations is a duty;[7] to give away surplus food is generosity. To forget yourself and to give away food as long as you will not starve yourself is a virtue. To hinder anyone against performing his duty is against the Law. To refuse to give away the leftovers of our food is greedy and extremely miserly. To refuse to deprive yourself in order to give away part of your food which you need is excusable. To deprive yourself of food, and to deprive your family to any extent, is ignoble, vile, and criminal. To be generous with property which you have acquired by unfair means is to aggravate the evil already committed, and it should be rewarded with criticism, not praise, since you are in fact giving away someone else's property, not your own. To give people their rightful part of your possessions is not generosity; it is a duty.

90 The definition of courage is to fight to the death in defense of religion, in defense of womanhood, of ill treated neighbours, of the oppressed who seek protection, or in defense of a lost fortune, honour which has been attacked, and other rights, against all adversaries, whether they be few or many. To do less than this would be cowardliness and weakness. To use up one's courage

---

7 ⬡ This sentence is the start of a separate point in Source D.

in fighting for the vanities of the world would be stupid recklessness. But it is even more stupid to devote your courage to fighting against right and duty, either in your own interest or for others. And even more stupid than all these, there are men whom I have seen who do not know to what cause to devote themselves; sometimes they fight Zayd on 'Amr's account, and sometimes they fight 'Amr on Zayd's account, sometimes both in the same day, exposing themselves needlessly to danger, hurtling towards hellfire, or running towards dishonour. About such people the Messenger of Allāh has warned, "There will come a time for men, when the one who kills will not know why he has killed, and his victim will not know why he was killed."[8]

91  The definition of continence is to turn away one's glance and all of one's organs of sense from forbidden objects. Everything other than this is debauchery. Anyone who goes further, and forbids himself what the Almighty has made lawful, is weak and powerless.

92  The definition of justice is to give spontaneously what is due and to know how to take what is your right. The definition of injustice is to take one's due and not give others their due. The definition of nobility of soul is to give spontaneously and with a good heart what is due to others, and to allow them their rights willingly; this is also virtue. All generosity is noble and virtuous, but not every noble act and every virtue is generous. Virtue is a more general term; generosity is more specific. Magnanimity is a virtue without being generosity. Virtue is a general prescription to which one adds a specific action.

93  One hour of neglect can undo a year of pious effort.

94  In the course of affairs, a mistake made by an individual is better than a just policy followed by the whole assembly of Muslims if they are not grouped under the leadership of one man. This is because the individual's mistake can be put right, but the correct views of the Muslim assembly will lead them to ignore something that may have been wrong, and they will be lost because of it.

---

[8]  ✣ Reported by Imam Muslim.

95　Fitnah's blossom does not bear fruit.[9]

96　I myself had faults, and I tried continually to correct them, by discipline, by studying the words of the Prophets عليهم السلام and also the words of the most virtuous sages among the ancients who are more advanced in morality and self-discipline, until Allāh helped me overcome most of my faults, thanks to His guidance and grace.

　　It is an act of perfect virtue, of self-discipline, a sign that one controls the truth, to confess such faults in order that one day someone may learn from them, if Allāh wills.

97　One of my faults was that I tended to an extreme of self-satisfaction when I was in the right and an extreme bad temper when I was in the wrong. Ever seeking to cure myself of this, I decided that I would never again display any irritations in my remarks, my actions, or my discussions. I renounced every kind of triumph that was not permitted, and I suffered under the heavy burden of this decision. I had enough patience to bear a dreadful affliction which nearly made me sick and an invalid. But I was not capable of overcoming my passion to always be in the right. It almost seemed that I did not really think this a fault, that I did not really think I should give up this attitude.

98　Another fault I had was an ungovernable propensity for sarcasm. What I decided to do about this was to refrain from anything that might irritate the person I was talking to. But I did allow myself to crack jokes, feeling that not to do so would have been narrow-minded and almost arrogant.

99　Another fault: extreme pride. My mind wrangled with my soul, knowing my defects, and argued so long and so successfully that my pride vanished

---

9　◌ The original translation reads, "In times of civil war, the blossom does not bear fruit." The original Arabic reads نوار الفتنة لا يعقد (Source D). Its meaning was expounded in vol. 1, p. 67, of *al-ʿIrāq fī aḥādīth wa āthār al-Fitan* (Dubai: Maktabah al-Furqān, 2004):

والمعنى: أنّ للفتنة مظهراً خادعاً في مبدئه، قد يستحسن الناس صورتها، ويعقدون الآمال عليها، ولكن سرعان ما تموت وتتلاشى، مثل الزهرة التي تموت قبل أنْ تتفتح وتعطي ثمرتها.

completely, leaving no trace, thanks be to Allāh. Moreover, I set myself to despise myself absolutely and to be a model of humility.

100  Another of my defects was that I suffered from trembling caused by my youthfulness and the weakness of my limbs. I forced myself to make it stop, and it disappeared.

101  Another fault: a love of great fame and glory. To deal with this defect, I decided to renounce everything which was forbidden by religion, Allāh helping with the rest, because if the soul remains under the control of reason even its irritability can become a virtue and be regarded as a praiseworthy disposition.

102  I used to feel extreme repugnance for the company of women on any occasion, and this made me difficult to get on with. I seem to have been struggling forever against this immoderate feeling, which I know to be bad from the problems it has caused me. Allāh help me.

103  I had two faults which the Almighty has kept private and helped me to fight and overcome by His goodness. One has completely disappeared, all praise to Him for this. In this case, good luck seems to have been on my side: as soon as this fault rears its head I hasten to stifle it. But the other fault has tormented me for a long time. When its waves came sweeping over me, my veins would throb and this fault would be on the point of reappearing; but Allāh has allowed me to hold back by one of the manifestations of His goodness and it has now disappeared.

104  I used to persist in bearing extreme grudges; I have been enabled to conceal and hide this with the help of the Almighty and to avoid the manifestation of all its effects. But I have never been able to stamp it out completely, nor have I ever found it possible to make friends with anyone who has acted in a truly hostile way towards me.

105  Mistrust itself is regarded by some as an absolute fault. This is not so, unless it leads the person who feels it to commit deeds not allowed by religion,

or to adopt behaviour which is unsocial. In other cases, mistrust can be steadfastness, and steadfastness is a virtue.

106  As for the reproach made to me by ignorant adversaries who say that I put no value on anyone who disagrees with me when I believe that I am in the right, and that I would never act in concert with the ones I contradict even if they amounted to the entire human population on the face of the earth, and that I place no value on conforming with the people of my country in many of the customs or costume which they have adopted for no particular reason – this independence is a quality which I regard as one of my most important virtues. There is nothing equal to it, and, upon my life, if I did not possess it (Allāh forbid), it would be this that I most longed for, and hoped for, and prayed for to Allāh Almighty. In fact, my advice to all who may hear my words is to behave in the same way. There is no benefit to be had from copying other people if their actions are vain and pointless. By doing so one annoys the Almighty, and disappoints one's mind [deludes oneself], causes suffering to one's soul and body, and takes upon one's shoulders an unnecessary yoke.

107  A man who knows nothing of the truth has reproached me for not caring about wrongs done to me, or even wrongs done to my friends, so that I do not even get annoyed if they are wronged in my presence.

108  My reply would be that anyone who has described me like that was speaking too hastily and needs to be more precise. When one speaks hastily one slips into using language that makes the bad not so bad and the good not so good. For example, "So-and-so is sleeping with his sister," would be an abominable thing to say and would horrify everyone who heard it, but if you explained that it is a matter of "his sister in Islam," it would be clear that it was hasty speaking that created the indecent and ugly aspect of the matter.

109  For myself, if I pretended not to feel hurt when I am attacked by someone, I would not be telling the truth, for it is natural to feel hurt in such a case, it is only human. But I have forced myself to show neither anger nor bad temper nor fury.

I manage to hold back an angry answer by preparing myself in advance. This I can do so thanks to the strength and power of Almighty Allāh. But if I have no time to prepare myself, I restrict myself to retaliating with cutting phrases – but not insults – and I attempt to say only what is true, and to express myself without anger or cruelty. I detest doing even this, except when it is absolutely necessary.

For example when I wish to stop a false rumor being spread – for most people love to pass on to anyone who will listen, hateful tidbits of gossip (which they attribute to a third person) – and nothing will stop them so effectively as this course of action. It stops them touting around calumnies which they attribute to others, and which serve no purpose except to corrupt consciences and to spread slander.

110 Furthermore, as for the man who is wronging me, there are two possibilities and two only. Either he is lying or telling the truth. If he is lying, then Allāh will surely make haste to allow me to refute him by his own tongue, for this man will go the way of all liars and will draw attention to my merit by falsely imputing bad things to me – for sooner or later – this will become clear to most of those who listen to him. If he is telling the truth, there are three possibilities and only one can be true. Perhaps I had been his associate in some business and had confided in him as one does with someone one relies on and trusts, and he would then be the most despicable sneak: I hardly need say more about such base villainy. Or, perhaps he may be criticizing in me something which he regards as a fault and which in fact is not. His ignorance is enough to make this obvious; it is he who should be accused, and not the one who he has criticized. Or, finally, he may be accusing me of a fault which I really do have. Having perceived one of my faults, he has let his tongue wag about it. If he is telling the truth, I deserve more blame than he does. In that case, I should be angry with myself, not with my critic, who is justified in his criticism.

111 As for my friends, I have not forbidden myself to defend them. But I do it gently, contenting myself with persuading the person who has slandered them in my presence to repent, urging him to reproach himself, to apologize,

to feel ashamed, and to take back what he said. I achieve this by following the method which consists of blaming the slanderers and telling them that it would be better to mind their own business and put their own houses in order rather than track down the faults of others. I go on to recall the merits of my friend, reproaching the critic for limiting himself to recalling his faults without mentioning his virtues, and saying to him, "He would never speak like that about you. He has a more generous spirit than you, and that is what you would not accept," or something similar. As for attacking the speaker, annoying him, irritating him, making him angry, in this way pushing him to increase the insults to my friend which I so dislike, this would make me guilty towards my friend because it would expose him to coarse and repeated insults which would be spread to the ears of those who had not heard them before and would give rise to further slander. Perhaps this would make me just as guilty towards myself, which would not suit my friend, because I should suffer insult and injury. For myself, I would not want my friend to defend me beyond the limits I have outlined. If he goes further, and goes to the point of injuring the one who is insulting me, he will push him to increase his attacks, to go even further, to attack him, or even my father, my mother, and his own parents, depending on how insolent and impudent the one who started it is. They might even come to blows, I should scorn him, because he had brought this upon me; I certainly would not be grateful to him. On the contrary I should be extremely cross with him. Allāh help us!

112　A man of prejudice who never stops to think has accused me of squandering my fortune. This is more hasty talk, which I would explain as follows: I only squander the portion which it would be against my religion to keep or would cast aspersion on my honour or would fatigue me. I consider that what I avoid of these three evils, however small, far outweighs the amount of fortune lost, even if it amounted to everything that the sun shines on.

113　The best gift that Allāh can give His servant is to endow him with justice and a love of justice, with truth and a love of truth [equity] above all else. To stamp out my evil tendencies, to do everything which is good according to religion and to the world, I have done only what I could. There is no strength and power except in Allāh Almighty. On the other hand, a man who has a natural tendency towards injustice and who finds it easy to act unjustly, a man who has tendency to transgress and enjoys doing it, let him despair of ever improving or of amending his nature. Let him realize that he will not succeed, neither in religion nor in good conduct.

114 As for vanity, envy, falsehood, and treachery, I have absolutely no experience of them from my nature. It seems that I have no merit for avoiding them since all my being spurns them. Thanks for this be rendered to Allāh, Lord of the Worlds.

115 One of the defects of the love of renown is that it cancels out the value of good deeds, if the man performing them likes them to be spoken of. This makes him almost impious because he is working for something other than Allāh. This defect removes all the value from virtues because the man affected by it is hardly trying at all to do good for the sake of good, but for love of renown.

116 There is no worse blame than that of a man who praises a quality in you that you do not have, thereby drawing attention to its absence.

117 There is no better praise than that of a man who reproaches you for a fault that you do not have, thereby drawing attention to your merit, and he gives you your revenge on him by exposing himself to rebuttal and the reproach of having slandered you.

118 If one knew one's imperfections, one would be perfect. Since no creature is exempt from faults, happy the man whose defects are few and unimportant.

119 The thing that happens most often is something unexpected. Steadfastness consists of preparing yourself for as much as can be foreseen. Glory be to the One who has so arranged it in order to show mankind man's powerlessness and his need for his Creator, the Almighty.

Chapter Six

# *Brothers, Friends, and Advice*

120  Anyone who criticizes you cares about your friendship. Anyone who makes light of your faults cares nothing about you.

121  Criticizing a friend is like melting an ingot:[1] it will either become refined or it will disappear.

122  A friend who conceals a secret which concerns you is more disloyal towards you than one who tells a secret of yours. For the one who tells your secret is simply betraying you, but the one who conceals one from you is betraying you and also mistrusting you.

123  Do not try to be friends with those who scorn you. You will gain nothing from it but deception and shame.

124  Do not scorn those who try to be friends with you; to do so is a form of injustice and it would be failing to respond to their kindness, and this is bad.

125  Anyone who is forced to mix with men should on no account tell his companion everything that passes through his mind. When he leaves him, he must always behave as if he were a desperate enemy. When he wakes up each morning he should always expect his friends to betray him and do evil, expect them to behave exactly like his sworn enemies. If nothing of the sort

---

[1]  *ingot*: as *ingot-copper, ingot-gad, ingot-holder, ingot-mould, ingot-silver, ingot-steel,* etc. *ingot iron,* iron which contains too little carbon to temper and is nearly pure by industrial standards, differing from wrought iron in containing no slag.

happens, he should praise Allāh; if it does, then at least he will prepared and the shock will be less. For myself, I tell you I had a friend who had sworn friendship, sincere pure friendship, for bad times or good, for richer or poorer, in anger and in satisfaction. This friend changed his attitude towards me, in a most hateful way, after twelve years of perfect friendship, and for an absolutely futile reason which I would never have believed could influence such a man. He has never reconciled with me since, and this has made me very sad for many years.

However, one should not do bad things and follow the example of wicked men and traitors.

126 On the contrary, we should learn from this example the path that we should take. It is perilous and difficult to follow and a man would do well to advance as carefully as the pin-tailed sandgrouse,[2] more cautiously than the magpie,[3] until he turns off the road trodden by mankind and makes his way towards his Lord. This road leads to victory, so we are told by religion and also by the world. The man who follows it will keep the pure intention of healthy souls who are true to their promises, men without guile[4] and trickery. He will possess the virtues of the elect and the characters of the virtuous. Moreover, he will feel as safe as the worst deceivers, as free from care as the evildoers, as the most wicked and cunning people.

127 You should keep any secret that is confided to you, and not reveal it to any friend or stranger, even the man closest to you, if you are at all able to keep it. You should be true to everyone who trusts you, and do not yourself trust in anyone in affairs which you want to succeed except when absolutely nec-

---

[2]  ⬡ The pin-tailed sandgrouse is a robust, medium-sized bird about 31–39 cm (12–15 in.) in length. The general colouring is cryptic, a blend of barred and flecked olive green, brown, buff, yellow, grey, and black. The underparts and the feathered legs are dull white. The nominate race, *Pterocles alchata*, breeds in Iberia and southern France. (Wikipedia)

[3]  *magpie*: A common European bird, *Pica caudata*, of the family Corvidæ, having a long pointed tail and black-and-white plumage. It is well known for its noisy chatter, and is often taught to speak; its habits of pilfering and hoarding are proverbial, and it is popularly regarded as a bird of ill omen.

[4]  *guile*: Insidious cunning, deceit, treachery.

essary, and even then you should stop and think again and make a personal effort and draw strength from Allāh.

128   Be generous with your superfluous possessions and strength to help others, whether they ask you or not, and to help anyone who needs you and whom you are able to help, even if he does not expressly come to you for help.

129   Do not expect any help in return from anyone except Allāh, the Almighty and Great. As you go on your way always remember that the first person you help will be the first to do harm and turn against you. Indeed, because of their profound jealousy, men of bad character detest those that help them when they see that the latter are better off.

130   [In your social life] treat every human being as graciously as you can. If someone comes to you with defects and problems such as arise in the normal course of life, do not let them know that you do not like them. In this way you shall live in peace and quiet.

131   When you give advice, do not give it only on condition that it will be taken. Do not intercede only on the condition that your intercession is accepted; do not make a gift only on the condition that you will be recompensed. Do it only in order to practise virtue, and to do what you should do when giving advice, interceding, and being generous.

132   The definition of friendship: [it is the middle point] between two extremes.[5] What makes one friend sad makes the other sad too. What makes one happy makes the other happy too. Any relationship less than this is not friendship. Anyone who answers to this description is a friend. A man may be the friend of someone who is not his friend for a man can love someone who hates him. This is the case above all with fathers and their sons, brother and brother, husband and wife, and all those in whom friendship has become

---

[5]   This alludes to the theory of Plato and Aristotle taken up by Cicero and adopted by Ibn Ḥazm: virtue is a happy medium between excess and defect; see 294, where Ibn Ḥazm tells us which are the two extremes of which friendship is the happy medium (see also 308); they are excessive attachment and excessive hatred.

burning love. Not every friend is a counsellor although every counsellor, by giving advice shows himself to be a friend.

133 The definition of advice is that the man giving it feels bad about what harms his friend, whether the latter feels good or bad about it, and he feels happy about what is good for him, whether his friend is happy or unhappy about it. This is the added factor which a counsellor has which goes beyond the limit of simple friendship.

134 The highest aim of friendship – and there is nothing higher than this – is to have all things in common, one's own person, one's belongings, without any constraint, and to prefer one's friend to every other being. If I had not known Muẓaffar and Mubārak, the two masters of Valencia, I should have thought that such a sentiment had disappeared in our times. But I have never seen any two other men draw so deeply on all the joys of friendship, despite events which would have separated other men.

135 There is no virtue which so much resembles a vice as the faculty of having many friends and acquaintances. But it is really a perfect virtue, made up of various qualities, since friends are only gained by tolerance, generosity, patience, loyalty, signs of affection, shared feelings, and moderation. It is important to protect one's friends, teach them what one knows, and to win over them by every kind of praiseworthy action.

We do not mean mercenaries, or those who follow us in our days of glory. They are thieves of the title of friendship; they deceive friendship. You think that they are friends but they are not. The proof is that they abandon you when fortune abandons you. Nor do we mean those who make friends for a particular purpose, nor do we mean drinking companions, not those who gang together to commit crimes or villainy, to attack people's honour, to satisfy their unhealthy curiosity, or for any other useless objective. These are not friends at all. The proof is that they speak evil of each other, and that they disperse as soon as the evil interests which brought them together are finished. We only mean to speak of those pure friends who unite only in the love of Allāh, either to help each other to make some real virtue triumph or to taste the pleasures of the only true kind of friendship.

If one commits the fault of having too many friends, there is the difficulty of keeping them all happy, the dangers of associating with them, the duties which fall on us when they are subjected to trials (for if you betray them or let them down, you will be criticized and blamed; but if on the other hand you are true to them, you will harm yourself to the extent that you could lose your own life, and this choice is the only one acceptable to the virtuous man if he wishes to be true to his friendship); if one thinks of the worries which we have from the misfortunes which come upon them or which come upon us because of them: death, separation, betrayal of one among them, one will see that the joy brought by these friends is outweighed by the painful sadness which they cause.

136 There is nothing among the vices which is so like a virtue as the desire to be praised. Indeed, if someone sings our praises in our presence, we would be silly to believe it, knowing everything that the Tradition has taught us about flatterers. However, praise may be useful in encouraging someone to do fewer bad things and more good things. It may lead the person who hears it to desire to have a character similar to the one who has been praised. Thus, I feel that the following anecdote has the ring of truth: one of the great rulers of the world met one of those people who spread evil wherever they go and who are said to have done evil things, and he received him with praise. He had heard his praises sung everywhere, he said; on every side people spoke of nothing but his good deeds and his generosity. After this the criminal could not possibly do wrong!

137 Certain kinds of advice are difficult to distinguish from slander for anyone who hears a man criticising someone else unjustly or unfairly and conceals it from the person who is the object of this unjust and wicked statement, by doing this is so unjust and to be blamed. Moreover, if he breaks it to him bluntly, he may bring more trouble upon the spiteful critic than the latter really deserved. This would be unfair to him, for it is not fair to punish ill-doers beyond the measure of their unjust deed. It is difficult for anyone except a very intelligent man to cope with this situation.

138 The solution to be adopted by the intelligent man in such a situation is

to protect the victim against the slanderer, and no more, and not inform him what the latter said; this is to prevent him going to the slanderer and getting into more trouble. As for sly tricks, one should protect the victim, but nothing more than that.

139 Giving information consists of reporting to someone something one has heard which in no way harms the person one tells it to, strength is from Allāh.

140 Advice can be given twice. The first time is prescribed as a religious duty. The second time is a reminder and a warning. If you repeat the advice a third time it becomes a remonstrance[6] and a reprimand. After that you have to slap and punch and perhaps try even more serious methods which may cause harm and damage. Certainly, it is only in questions of religious practices that it is permissible to repeat advice incessantly, whether the listener accepts it or gets irritated, whether the advisor suffers from it or not. When you give advice, give it softly, do not shout it out; use hints, do not speak openly unless you are advising someone who is determined not to understand. Then explanations would be essential. Do not give advice only on condition that it is followed. Otherwise you are a tyrant, not an adviser; you are demanding obedience, you are not allowing religious feeling and brotherly spirit their due. Neither reason nor friendship gives you the right to insist. It is rather the right that a ruler has over his subjects or a master over his slaves.

141 Do not burden your friend except with as much as you would be willing to sacrifice for him. For if you demand more than that, you would be an oppressor. Do not gain except on the condition of loss, and do not take up a position except on the condition that you will leave it. Otherwise, you will harm yourself and taint your own reputation.[7]

---

6 From *remonstrate*: To urge strong reasons *against* a course of action, to protest *against*; to expostulate *with* a person, *on* or *upon* an action.

7 ⚙ The original translation reads, "Do not ask your friend more than you yourself are prepared to give. To ask for more is to abuse his friendship. Do not gain except when there is a possibility of losing. Do not take power unless you know how to set it aside again. Otherwise, you will harm yourself and your behaviour will be detestable." The edit is literally closer to the original Arabic.

142  If you find excuses for selfish and greedy men and shut your eyes to their faults, you are not displaying humanity or virtue. On the contrary, it is a base and feeble thing to do which encourages them to continue in their bad attitudes, it applauds and supports them in their wicked actions. Such indulgence would only be humane when displayed towards the just who are quick to pardon and to act unselfishly. In that case it is an obligation for a good man to behave in the same way towards them, above all if they have an urgent need of such tolerance, and if it is more necessary for them.

143  One might retort, "According to what you say, we should stop being tolerant, we should stop turning a blind eye when it is a question of our friends. Friends, enemies, and strangers would all be treated exactly the same; this cannot be right." Our reply would be – and may Allāh help us succeed – nothing but encouragement towards tolerance and unselfishness.

144  You should turn a blind eye not on [the faults of] the greedy but only on [those of] a true friend. If you wish to know how you should act in this matter, how you can keep on the path of truth: if there is a situation where one of two friends needs to be unselfish for the other's sake, each of two friends should examine the problem and see which of them is in the most urgent need, the most pressing circumstances. Friendship and humanity then impose on the other the obligation to be unselfish. If he does not, he is greedy, avid, and deserves no indulgence since he is acting neither like a friend nor like a brother.

If the two find themselves in equal need, in equal straits, true friendship would require that they race each other to be the more unselfish. If they behave like this, they are both friends. If one of them hastens to be unselfish and the other does not, and if this is what usually happens, the second is not a friend and there is no need to be friendly towards him. But if he would hasten to sacrifice himself in other circumstances then this is a pair of true friends.

145  If there is someone in need whom you wish to help, whether the initiative came from him or from you, do no more than he expects of you, not what

you might personally wish to do. If you overstep the mark, you will deserve not thanks but blame from him and from others, and you will attract hostility, not friendship.

146   Do not repeat to your friend things that will make him unhappy and which it would not benefit him to know. That would be the action of a fool. Do not hide from him anything that would cause him loss not to know. That would be the action of a wicked person.

147   Do not be pleased if someone praises you for a quality which you do not have; on the contrary, be very sorry because it will bring to public attention that you lack it. To sing such praises is to mock and poke fun, and only an idiot or an imbecile would be pleased. Do not be sorry if someone criticizes you for a fault that you do not have; on the contrary, you should be pleased because your merit will be brought to public attention.

148   On the other hand, you should be pleased to possess a praiseworthy quality, whether anyone actually praises you for it or not, and you should be sorry to have a blameworthy fault, whether anyone actually criticizes you for it or not.

149   Anyone who hears bad things said about the wife of his friend must on no account tell him, particularly if the person who said them was a slanderer or libeller[8] or notorious gossip, one of those people who try to draw attention away from their own faults by increasing the number of people like themselves; this often happens.

As a general rule, it is best to stick to the truth. Now, in this case, you cannot know whether the statements are true or false, but you do know that it is a grave sin against your religion to hold such opinions. However, if you perceive that the same thing is being said from several gossips, not just one, or if you are able to verify that the statement is well founded, even if you cannot put your friend in a position to observe what you have observed,

---

[8]   *libeller*: One who libels another; one who publishes a libel or libels. *Libel*: (n.) In popular use: Any false and defamatory statement in conversation or otherwise. (v.) To make libellous accusations or statements; to spread defamation.

then you should tell him everything, privately and tactfully. You should say something like "There are many women…" or "Look after your house, teach your family, avoid this, mind that…"

If he takes your advice and is put on his guard, he will have profited from the chance. If you notice that he takes no precautions and does not worry about anything, you must control yourself, not say a word, and remain friends, for the fact that he has not believed what you have told him does not oblige you to break with him. But if, having been in a position to observe some definite proof, you are able to put your friend in a position to see some identical proof, it is your duty to tell him and to make him face the whole truth. If he changes his attitude, that is good. But if he will not change his attitude, you should shun his friendship, because this would be vile man with no virtue and no noble aspirations.

150  The fact that a man enters a house secretly is proof enough that he means ill. The same is true of a woman who enters a man's house secretly. It would be stupid to require further proof. You should run from such a woman or at least separate. Anyone who keeps such a woman as a wife after all this is a cuckold.[9]

151  Men can be divided into seven categories according to certain traits of their characters. Some praise you to your face and criticize you behind your back. This is the characteristic feature of hypocrites and slanderers; it is common, mostly among men. Others criticize you to your face and behind your back. This is characteristic of slanderers who are powerful and insolent. Some men flatter you to your face and behind your back. This is the mark of flatterers and social climbers. Others again criticize you to your face and praise you behind your back. This is characteristic of fools and imbeciles. Virtuous people take care neither to praise nor to criticize you in your presence. Either they praise you in your absence, or they refrain from criticizing you.

---

[9]  ✦ The original translation reads, "Anyone who kept her with him would be a virtual go-between," but this didn't reflect the original Arabic, وَمُسِكُهَا لَا يَبْعُدُ عَنِ الدِّيَاثَة... (See p. 29 of Source A and no. 117, p. 126 of Source B).

Slanderers who are not hypocrites or ignorant say nothing to your face and criticize you in your absence. As for those who want a quiet life, they take care that they neither praise you nor criticize you, whether you are present or absent. We have seen these different types of individuals for ourselves, and we have tested the categories and found them to be true.

152 When you give advice, find a private place and speak gently. Do not say that somebody else has said the criticisms that you address to your companion, that would be to speak ill. If your phrase your advice bluntly, you will annoy and discourage. The Almighty has said, ﴿فَقُولَا لَهُ قَوْلًا لَّيِّنًا...﴾ , «Speak to him courteously,» (Quran 20:44) And the Prophet said, "Do not discourage him." If you are advising someone, and you insist on seeing your advice taken, you are doing wrong since you could be mistaken and you would be insisting on him accepting your error and rejecting the truth.

153 Everything has its use. Thus, I have profited greatly from mixing with the ignorant. This has inspired my inward self, it has sparked off my spirit, it has sharpened my mind, it has driven me to action. It has given rise to written works of some value. If the ignorant had not roused something deep within myself, if they had not woken something that lay hatching in me, I would not have thrown myself into writing these works.

154 Do not blind yourself to a friend by taking a wife from his family; do not sign a contract with him. We have never known these two acts to result in anything but rupture, where ignorant people would expect the ties of friendship to be strengthened. Not so, and the reason is that the two acts force each party to press his own interests to the advantage of others. When there is a clash of individual interests, quarrels result, quarrels bring about an alteration in affections. The firmest alliance is one between two people who are already related, because the fact that they are already related forces them to bear the union, even if they are very unhappy, since they are joined by an unbreakable tie, that of their common origin, which nature obliges them to defend and protect.

Chapter Seven

# *Different Kinds of Love*

155    I have been asked to focus on what there is to say about love, and the different kinds of love. All the different kinds of love belong to the same family. Love is characterized by longing for the loved one, horror of separation, hope of having one's love reciprocated. It has been suggested that the sentiment varies according to its object. But the object varies only according to the lover's desires, according to whether they are on the increase, the decrease, or are vanishing altogether. Thus, love felt for Allāh Almighty is perfect love; that which unites beings in the quest for the same ideal, the love of a father, a son, parents, a friend, a sovereign, a wife, a benefactor, a person in whom one has placed one's hopes, a lover, all is generally the same, all is love, but there are different species as I have just listed, differing by the amount of love inspired by what the loved one is able to give of itself. Thus love can take different forms: we have seen men die broken-hearted because of their sons exactly as a lover might have his heart broken by his loved one. We have heard of a man who burnt with such fear of Allāh, with such love, that he died of it. We know that a man can be as jealous of them as a lover is of his mistress.

156    The least that the lover can desire of the loved one is to win her esteem, her attention, and to approach her – not daring to expect more. This is how far those aspire who love each other for Allāh Almighty.

157    The next stage is when desire grows as time is spent together, in conversation, and interest is shown by one another. This is the level of the love of a man towards his prince, his friend, or his own brother.

158   But the height of what a lover may wish from the loved one is to take her in his arms when he desires her. That is why we see a man who is passionately fond of his wife trying different positions in making love, and different places, so as to feel that he possesses her more completely. It is in this category that we should put caresses and kisses. Some of these desires may arise in a father towards his child and may drive him to [express them] in kisses and caresses.

159   Everything that we have just mentioned is uniquely the function of [extreme] desire. When for some reason, the desire for some object is suppressed, the soul is driven towards a different object of desire.

160   Thus we find that the man who believes in the possibility of seeing Allāh Almighty longs for it, has a great yearning for it and will never be satisfied with anything less since it is that which he desires. On the other hand, a man who does not believe in it does not aspire to this ecstasy and does not wish for it, having no desire for it. He is content to bow to divine will and to go to the mosque. He has no other ambition.

161   We have observed that a man who is legally able to marry his close relatives is not satisfied with favours which would satisfy someone who is not permitted to marry them. His love does not stop at the same point as the love of a man who is forbidden by law to love them. Those, such as Magians and Jews, who are permitted to marry their own daughters and nieces, do not curb their love at the same point as a Muslim does. On the contrary, they feel the same love towards their daughters or to their nieces as a Muslim does to a woman he will sleep with. One never sees a Muslim desiring his close relatives in this way, even if they are more beautiful than the sun itself, even if he is the most debauched[1] and the most amorous[2] of men. And if, very exceptionally, it should happen, it would be only among the impious, who do not feel the constraint of the religion, and who allow themselves every lustful thought, and who find every gate of desire open to them. It cannot

---

[1]   *debauched*: Seduced or corrupted from duty or virtue; depraved or corrupt in morals; given up to sensual pleasures or loose living; dissolute, licentious.

[2]   *amorous*: Of persons: Inclined to love; habitually fond of the opposite sex.

be guaranteed that a Muslim might not love his cousin so excessively that his love became a passion and overstepped the affection which he bore towards his daughter and niece, even if the cousin was not so beautiful as they.  In fact he might desire favours from his cousin which he would never expect from his daughter or his niece. On the other hand, a Christian will treat his cousin with equal respect, for he is not permitted to desire her. But [unlike a Muslim] he does not have to restrain himself with anyone who shared a wet nurse with him, since he may desire her without offending the laws of his religion.

162   We now see the truth of what we said earlier: love in all its manifestations forms one single generic family, but its species vary according to the different objects of its desire.

163   Having said this, human nature is the same everywhere but different customs and religious beliefs have created apparent differences.

164   We do not say that desire has an influence only on love. We would say that it is the cause of all kinds of cares, even those which concern one's fortune and social position. Thus it may be observed that a man who sees the death of his neighbour, or of his maternal uncle, his friend, his cousin, his great-uncle, his nephew, his maternal grandfather or his grandson, having no claim on their property, does not fret because it has escaped him, however large and considerable their fortunes might be, because he had no expectation of them.  But as soon as a distant member of his father's family dies, or one of his remotest clients, he begins to covet their belongings. And with the coveting comes crowding in anxiety, regret, anger, and great sorrow if some tiny part of their fortune escapes him.

165   It is the same with one's position in society: a man who belongs to the lowest social class does not fret if he is not consulted when someone else is given charge of the affairs of the land. He does not fret if someone else is promoted or demoted. But as soon as he begins to feel an ambition to better himself, it provokes so much worry, anxiety, and anger that it could make him lose his soul, his world, and his position in the hereafter [lose his soul here and

in the hereafter]. Thus covetousness is the cause of all humiliation and every kind of anxiety. It is a wicked and despicable kind of behaviour.

166 The opposite of covetousness is disinterest. This is a virtuous quality which combines courage, generosity, justice, and intelligence. A disinterested man is truly intelligent because he understands the vanity of covetousness and prefers disinterest. His courage gives birth to a greatness of spirit which makes him disinterested. His natural generosity stops him fretting about property which is lost to him. His equitable nature makes him love reserve and moderation in his desires. Thus, disinterest is composed of these four qualities, just as covetousness, its opposite, is composed of the four opposite faults, that is, cowardice, greed, injustice, and ignorance.

Greed is a kind of covetousness which would like to possess everything; it is insatiable and ever increasing in its demands. If there were no such thing as covetousness, nobody would ever humiliate himself to anybody else. Abū Bakr ibn Abī al-Fayyāḍ has told me that "'Uthmān ibn Muḥāmis [d. AH 356 / 966 CE] inscribed upon the door of his house in Ecija [in Seville], 'O 'Uthmān, do not covet anything.' "[3]

## 7.1   Other Species of this Kind

167 A man made unhappy by the presence of a person he detests is like a man made unhappy by the absence of the person he loves. There is nothing to choose between them.

168 When a lover wishes to forget, he is sure to be able to do so. This wish is always granted.

169 If you treat the person you live with with respect, he will treat you with respect.

---

[3]   ✧ The original translation reads, "'Uthmān covets nothing." The Arabic in Source D is يا عثمان لا تطمع. Thus, the edit is closer in the sense of it being a reminder instead of a proclamation.

170  The man who is unhappy in love is the one who is racked by a passion
     for one whom he can keep locked away and with whom he may be united
     without incurring the wrath of Allāh or the criticism of his fellow men. All
     is well when the two lovers agree in loving each other. For love to run its
     course freely, it is essential that the two do not feel bored, for that is a bad
     feeling which gives rise to hatred. Perfect love would be if destiny forgot
     the two lovers while they were enjoying each other. But where could that
     happen except in Paradise? Only there can love be sure of shelter, for that is
     the home of everlasting stability. Otherwise, in the world, such feelings are
     not protected from misfortunes, and we go through life without ever tasting
     pleasure to the fullest.

171  When jealousy dies, you may be sure that love has also died.

172  Jealousy is a virtuous feeling which is made of courage and justice; truly, a
     just man hates to infringe the sacred rights of others, and hates to see others
     infringe his own sacred rights. When courage is inborn in a person, it gives
     rise to a grandeur of spirit which abhors injustice.

173  A man whose fortunes I have followed during these times told me once that
     he himself had never known jealousy until he was racked by love. Only then
     did he feel jealous. This man was corrupt by nature, he was a bad character,
     but nevertheless he was perspicacious[4] and generous.

174  There are five stages in the growth of love: first is to think someone pleasant,
     that is, someone thinks of someone else as being nice or is charmed by their
     character. This is part of making friends. Then there is admiration, i.e. the
     desire to be near the person that one admires. Then there is close friendship
     when you miss the other one terribly when they are absent. Then there is
     amorous[5] affection when you are completely obsessed with the loved one.
     In the special vocabulary of love this is called *'ishq*, "the slavery of love." Fi-
     nally, there is passion, when one can no longer sleep, eat, or think. This can

---

4  *perspicacious*: Of persons, their faculties, etc.: Of clear or penetrating mental vision or discernment.
5  *amorous*: Of persons: Inclined to love; habitually fond of the opposite sex.

make you ill to the point of delirium[6] or even death. Beyond this, there is absolutely no place where love ends.

175 We used to think that passion was found more often among lively and emotional women. But our experience has shown that this is not the case. Passion is found most often among calm women, as long as their calmness is not the placidity[7] of stupidity.

---

[6] *delirium*: A disordered state of the mental faculties resulting from disturbance of the functions of the brain, and characterized by incoherent speech, hallucinations, restlessness, and frenzied or maniacal excitement.

[7] *placidity*: The quality of being placid; mildness, calmness, tranquillity, peacefulness.
*placid*: Pleasing, agreeable, welcome. (now mostly obsolete in this sense)

Chapter Eight

# *Physical Beauty*

When I was asked to examine this matter, this is how I responded:

176 Gracefulness consists of delicate features, supple movements, graceful gestures, a soul in harmony with the form which fate has given it, even where there is no visible beauty.

177 Allure is beauty of each feature regarded separately. But someone whose features are beautiful when considered separately can still appear cold and be without piquantness,[1] charm, seductiveness, or grace.

178 Seductiveness is the aura of the visible parts; it also goes by the name of elegance and attractiveness.

179 Charm is a certain something which has no other name to explain it. It is the soul which perceives it, and everyone knows what it is as soon as they see it. It is like a veil covering the face, a shining light which draws all hearts to it so that all agree that it is beautiful, even if it is not accompanied by beautiful features. Anyone who sees it is seduced, charmed, enslaved, and yet if you looked at each feature separately you would find nothing special. It might be said that there is a certain unknown something which you see when you look into the soul. This is the supreme kind of beauty. However, tastes do differ. Some prefer seductiveness, others prefer gracefulness. But I have never met anyone who preferred allure as such.

---

[1] *piquant*: That acts upon the mind as a piquant sauce, or the like, upon the palate; that stimulates or excites keen interest or curiosity; pleasantly stimulating or disquieting.

180  We call beauty piquant when there is a combination of some of these qualities.

Chapter Nine

# *Practical Morality*

181  Fickleness, which is a fault, consists of switching from one way of life which is forced and senseless, to another way of life which is equally forced and senseless; from one absurd state to an equally absurd state for no good reason.

182  But a man who will adopt habits which suit his capabilities and his needs, and who will reject everything that is of no use to him [will be drawing on] one of the best sources of good sense and wisdom.

183  The Prophet  – the model of all goodness, whose character was praised by Allāh, in whom Allāh gathered together the most diverse and perfect virtues, and whom He kept from sin – was in the habit of visiting the sick, accompanied by his friends. They went to the boundaries of Madīnah on foot, wearing neither boots or sandals, nor hats or turbans. He wore clothes woven from the hair of wild beasts when he had them, or he might equally likely be wearing embroidered cloth if he had it, never wearing anything unnecessary and never forgetting anything necessary, content with what he had and doing without whatever he did not have. Sometimes he would ride a fine mule or he would ride a horse bareback or a camel or a donkey, with a friend riding behind him. Sometimes he ate dates without bread, sometimes dry bread, sometimes he ate roast lamb, fresh melon, or *ḥalwá*, taking as much as needed and sharing out the surplus, or leaving what he did not need and not forcing himself to take more than he needed. He was never angry when he found himself alone fighting for a cause, and he let nothing prevent him from anger when it was a question of Allāh, the Almighty.

184 The perseverance which consists of keeping one's word and the perseverance which is nothing but obstinacy[1] are so alike that they can only be told apart by someone who knows what different characters are like. The difference between the two kinds of perseverance is that obstinacy clings to error. Its actions are the actions of someone who persists in doing what he has decided upon when he knows that he is wrong, or when he does not know for sure whether he is right or wrong. Such obstinacy is wrong. The opposite of obstinacy is fairness. As for the kind of perseverance which consists of keeping one's word, its actions are the actions of someone who is right, or who believes himself to be right, not having seen any reason not to believe this. This quality is worthy of praise, and its opposite is inconstancy.[2] Only the first of the two kinds of perseverance [obstinacy] is wrong, because it makes you lose the habit of thinking about a matter once it has been decided, and you stop wondering whether the decision is right or wrong.

185 Good sense is defined as the practise of obedience to Allāh and the practice of piety and virtues. This definition implies avoidance of rebellion and vices. Allāh has stated this clearly more than once in His book (the Quran), emphasizing that anyone who disobeys Him is acting unreasonably. Speaking of certain people, the Almighty has said, ﴾وَقَالُوا۟ لَوْ كُنَّا نَسْمَعُ أَوْ نَعْقِلُ مَا كُنَّا فِىٓ أَصْحَٰبِ ٱلسَّعِيرِ ۝﴿ «They will say: if we had listened, if we had understood, we would not be among the damned,» (Quran 67:10) and He has confirmed their words as true by saying, ﴾فَٱعْتَرَفُوا۟ بِذَنۢبِهِمْ فَسُحْقًا لِّأَصْ﴿ «They have recognized their own sins, so misfortune be to the damned.» (Quran 67:11)

186 Stupidity is defined as the practice of disobedience to Allāh and the practice of vices.

187 As for going wild, throwing stones at people, not knowing what one is saying, that is lunacy and excess of bile.

---

[1] *obstinacy*: The quality or condition of being obstinate; inflexibility of temper or purpose; pertinacity, obduracy, stubbornness; persistency. Rarely in neutral or good sense.

[2] *inconstancy*: Of persons (or things personified, as Fortune): Fickleness of conduct or purpose; changeableness of character or disposition; unsteadfastness.

188 Stupidity is opposite of good sense, as we have shown above; and there is no middle point between good sense and stupidity unless it is ineptitude.[3]

189 The definition of ineptitude is to work and speak in a way that neither serves religion nor the world nor a healthy morality. This is neither disobedience to Allāh nor obedience, it does not bring anybody else to such acts, it is neither a virtue nor a harmful vice. It consists only of drivelling[4] and rambling about doing pointless things. According to whether these actions are frequent or rare, the person should be treated as more or less inept. Moreover he may be inept in one matter, sensible in another, stupid in a third.

190 The opposite of madness is the ability to discern and the ability to make free use of sciences and technical knowledge. It is what the ancients called the "faculty of reasoning." There is no middle point between these two extremes.

191 As for the art of conducting one's affairs and flattering people by means that might win their good will and save a situation, such as false dealing, perversion or any other bad practices, and as for the tricks which allow one to amass a fortune or to increase one's reputation or to achieve glory by means of a crime or every kind of base behaviour, these are not the works of good sense. Indeed, even those people who avowed that they had lost their senses and whose words Allāh confirmed as true when He said that they had lost their senses, knew very well how to conduct their worldly affairs, build up their fortunes, flatter their rulers, and protect their own standing. This characteristic is called astuteness, and the opposite of it is intelligence and honesty.

192 However, if in order to achieve these same ends, someone acted with reserve and dignity, this would be firmness. Its opposite is weakness or wasting.

193 To be serious, to know how to put each word in the right place, to preserve moderation in the way that you conduct your life, to show courtesy towards

---

[3] *ineptitude*: Want of aptitude; inaptness, unsuitableness, unfitness to or for something; incapacity.

[4] *drivelling*: Characterized by or given to silly childish talk or weak action; idiotic.

anyone who comes to you, that is called steadiness and is the opposite of ineptitude.

194    The virtue of keeping one's word is made up of fairness, generosity, and courage. Because a trustworthy man thinks it is unfair to deceive anyone who has put his trust in him or anyone who has done him a good deed, he acts with fairness. Because he wishes to help to repair the injustices of fate as quickly as possible, he acts with generosity. Because he has decided to bear without flinching all the likely consequences of his fidelity,[5] he is courageous.

195    Virtues have four roots which form all of virtue. They are: fairness or justice, intelligence, courage, and generosity.

196    Vices have four roots which are the basis of all faults and which are the opposite of the constituents of the virtues. They are: unfairness, ignorance, cowardice, and greed.

197    Honesty and temperance[6] are two kinds of fairness and generosity.

Here are some lines of my poetry dealing with morals. Abū Muḥammad Alī bin Aḥmad says:

The spirit is the foundation
     morals build the fortress upon it.
If the spirit does not adorn itself with
     knowledge, it will surely find itself in distress.
An ignorant person is surely blind
     and does not see where he is going.
If knowledge is not paired with justice,
     it is deceitful.
If justice is not paired with generosity,
     it is oppressive.

---

[5]   *fidelity*: The quality of being faithful; faithfulness, loyalty, unswerving allegiance to a person, party, bond, etc.

[6]   *temperance*: The practice or habit of restraining oneself in provocation, passion, desire, etc.; rational self-restraint. (One of the four cardinal virtues.)

Generosity depends on courage.
>Cowardice is deceitful.
Keep yourself in check if you are jealous.
>A jealous person has never yet committed adultery.
All these virtues are sublimated in piety.
>Truth spreads light when it is spoken.
It is from the roots of Good that springs vows
>[that bring us nearer to Allāh].

And here some other lines of poetry in my style:

The reins which control all the virtues are
>Justice, intelligence, generosity, and strength.
The other virtues are composed of these four.
>Anyone who possesses them is at the head of his people.
Likewise it is in the head that one finds
>The qualities of good sense that enable one to resolve all difficulties.

198 Disinterest as a human quality is a virtue which is made up of courage and generosity. The same is true of patience.

199 Magnanimity[7] is one kind of courage. It does not have an opposite.

200 Moderation is a virtue which is made up of generosity and fairness.

201 Ruthlessness arises from covetousness, and covetousness arises from envy. Envy arises from desire, and desire arises from injustice, greed, and ignorance.

202 Ruthlessness gives rise to great vices, such as servility,[8] theft, anger, adultery, murder, passions, and fear of poverty.

203 To beg for something that belongs to someone else stems from a tendency which is midway between ruthlessness and covetousness.

---

[7] *magnanimity*: Nobility of feeling; superiority to petty resentment or jealousy; generous disregard of injuries.

[8] *servility*: Mean submissiveness, degradingly obsequious demeanour, cringing.

204 If we make a distinction between ruthlessness and covetousness, it is only because ruthlessness reveals the covetousness that is hidden in the soul.

205 The art of dealing with people is a quality composed of magnanimity and patience.

206 Truthfulness is composed of justice and courage.

207 Anyone who comes to you with lies will go away with truths; that is to say, anyone who repeats to you lies which he attributes to a third person will make you beside yourself[9] with rage; you will respond to him, and your response is the truth that he will carry away. Therefore be careful not to behave like this, and only answer when you are certain about the provenance[10] of the lies.

208 There is nothing worse than falsehood. For how do you not regard a vice which has as one of its varieties disbelief or impiety itself? For all disbelief is falsehood. Falsehood is the genus and disbelief is one of its species. Falsehood arises from wickedness, cowardice, and ignorance. Truly, cowardice debases the soul. A liar has a vile soul which is far away from achieving greatness worthy of praise.

209 If we categorize people by the way of their speaking – and, remember, it is speech that distinguishes mankind from donkeys, dogs, and vermin – we can divide them into three groups: the first kind do not worry about what they pass on, they say everything that comes into their heads, without keeping to the truth or correcting mistakes, and this is the case with the majority of people. Another group speak in order to defend their own fixed opinions, or to protest against what they believe to be false, without trying to establish the truth, merely holding their ground. This is frequently the case, but it is not so serious as the first group. The third group makes use of language in the way of Allāh intended and this is more precious than red sulphur.

---

[9] *beside yourself*: In a state of extreme excitement or agitation. *They were beside themselves with glee.*

[10] *provenance*: The fact of coming from some particular source or quarter; origin, derivation.

210  Endless anxiety awaits a man who is goaded[11] or irritated by justice.

211  Two kinds of people live a life without care: one kind are extremely worthy of praise, the other kind are extremely worthy of criticism. The two kinds are those who care nothing for the pleasures of this world, and those who care nothing for *ḥayā'*, modesty.

212  To distance ourselves from the vanities of the world, it should suffice to remember that every night every man alive, in his sleep, forgets everything that worried him during the day, all his fears, all his hopes. He no longer remembers his children or his parents, glory or obscurity, high social responsibilities or unemployment, poverty or riches, nor catastrophes. Such a lesson should be sufficient for a thoughtful person.

213  One of the most marvellous arrangements in Allāh's world is that He has made the things that are most necessary also the most easily attainable, as can be seen in the case of water and the thing which is even more necessary (i.e. air). And the less essential a thing is, the rarer it is, as can be seen in the case of sapphires and things which are even less useful.

214  With all the worries, a man is like someone walking across a desert. Every time that he crosses a certain area, he sees other areas opening in front of him. Likewise, every time that a man gets something done, he finds other tasks piling up.

215  That man was right who said that the good have a hard time in this world. But the man who said that the good are at rest was also right. The good do suffer from all the evil that they see spread over everything, dominating it, and all the appearances of injustice which rear up between true justice and themselves. But their calmness comes from [their indifference to] all the vanities of this world which so worry the rest of mankind.

---

[11] *goad*: To assail or prick as with a goad; to irritate; to instigate or impel by some form of mental pain or annoyance; to drive by continued irritation *into* or *to* some desperate action or uncontrolled state of mind.

216 Take care not to agree with a wicked speaker, nor to help your contemporaries by doing anything which might harm you in this world or the next – however little – for you will reap nothing but regret, at a time when regret will not help you at all. The man you helped will not thank you. On the contrary, he will rejoice at your misfortune, or at least – you may be certain – he will be indifferent to the bad results [of your action] and your sad ending. But guard against contradicting the speaker and opposing your contemporaries to the extent that you harm yourself in this world or the next, however little. You will reap only loss, hostility, and enmity. You may even allow yourself to take sides, and you may suffer considerable trials which will be of no benefit [to you] whatsoever.

217 If you have to choose between annoying people or annoying the Almighty, and if there is no way out except either to run away from the Truth or to run away from the people, you should choose to annoy the people and run away from them, but do not annoy your Lord, do not run away from the Truth.[12]

218 You should imitate the Prophet ﷺ when he preached to the ignorant, the sinful, and the wicked. Anyone who preaches drily[13] and cheerlessly is doing wrong and is not applying the Prophet's method. Such preaching would usually only drive his audience to persist in their wicked ways, from obstinacy, anger, and rage against the insolent sermonizer. He would then have done bad with his talk, not good. But a man who exhorts in a friendly fashion, with a smile and with gentleness, putting on the appearance of offering advice and seeming to be speaking of a third person when he criticises the faults of the one he is speaking to, then his words reach farther and have more effect. But if they are not well received, he should go on to exhort or to appeal to the man's sense of shame, but only in private. And if [his advice] is still not taken, he should speak in the presence of someone who will make the sinner change. This is the practice which Allāh ordains when He commands

---

12 ☼ The original translation reads "…to run away from the right…" Truth seems like a closer translation to the original Arabic الى [Source D].

13 *drily*: Without emotion, sympathy, or cordiality, coldly, frigidly.

the use of قَوْلٌ لَّيِّنٌ "courteous terms." The Prophet  used not to address his listeners directly; instead, he would say to them, "What are they thinking of, the people who do such thing?…" He  praised gentleness, commended us to be tolerant and not to argue. He  varied his sermons so as not to be boring. And Allāh has said, ﴾وَلَوْ كُنتَ فَظًّا غَلِيظَ ٱلْقَلْبِ لَٱنفَضُّواْ مِنْ حَوْلِكَ﴿ «If you are harsh, and hard-hearted, they would have scattered from about you.» (Quran 3:159) Severity and hardness should not be used except to inflict the punishment ordained by Allāh. A man who has been given special authority to inflict such punishment must not be gentle.

219 Something which can also have a good effect in a sermon is to praise, in the presence of a wrongdoer, somebody who has acted differently. This is an incitement to behave better. I know no other benefit of the love of praise: a person who hears another being praised models himself on him. It is for this reason that we should tell stories of virtue and vice, so that anyone who hears them may turn away from the wicked deed that he hears others have done and accomplish the good deeds that he hears that others have done, thus learning from history.

220 I have considered everything that lives beneath the skies, I have reflected long upon it, and I have observed that everything that exists, whether animate or inanimate, has a natural tendency to build itself up by divesting the other species of their characteristics and investing them with his own. Thus, a virtuous man hopes that all mankind will become virtuous and the sinner hopes that all mankind will become sinful. One may observe that everybody who recalls a past action of their own which they incite others to imitate says, "I always do such and such." Someone with a doctrine wishes that everybody would agree with him. This phenomenon can also be seen among the elements: when some become stronger than others, they change them to their own substance: you can see how trees are formed, and how plants and trees are nourished by transforming water and the moisture in the soil to their own substance. For this may glory be given to Him who created and organized all things, there is no other Lord but He.

221 One of the most astonishing manifestations of Allāh's power is that [despite]

the great number of creatures that exist, you never see one so alike another that there is no difference between them. I asked a man who was very old and had reached his eighties whether he had ever seen in the past any form that resembled somebody nowadays to the point of being identical. "No," he replied, "on the contrary, every form has something distinctive about it." The same is true of everything that exists in the world. Whoever makes a study of various objects and of the bodies they make up, whoever makes a long and frequent examination of them, knows this, and is able to discern the differences and to distinguish one object from another thanks to the nuances which the soul can perceive but words cannot express. Glory then to the Almighty, the Omniscient, whose power is infinite.

222  A curious thing in this world is to see people allow themselves to be dominated by perverse hopes which will bring them nothing but trouble in the short term and anxiety and sin in the long term. For example, one person will hope for a rise in the price of foodstuffs, a rise which might be fatal for some people. But, even if one has a certain interest in something happening, the fact that one hopes for it does not make it happen before its time, and nothing will happen that Allāh has not decided. If he had wished for the good and the prosperity of other people, he would have speeded his own reward, and achieved peace of mind and virtue, without fatiguing himself at all. Be amazed at the useless corruption of these characters!

Chapter Ten

# *Treatment of Corrupt Character*

223   A man who is subject to pride should think of his faults.  If he is proud of his virtues, he should seek out what is mean in his character.  And if his faults are so well hidden from him that he thinks he has none, let him know that his misfortune will last forever, that he is the worst of men, that he has the worst faults of all, and is the least perceptive.

224   In the first place, he is weak in mind and ignorant.  No fault is worse then these two, for a wise man is one who sees his own faults, fights against them, and tries to overcome them.  A fool ignores them because he has little knowledge and discernment and his thoughts are feeble, possibly because he takes his faults to be good qualities, and there is nothing on earth worse than this.

225   There are many who boast of having committed adultery, homosexuality [acts of child abuse], theft, and other sins, and are proud of these stains and of the aptitudes that they deployed in these shameful acts.

226   Know well that nobody upon earth is free of all faults except the Prophets, may Allāh bless them.

227   A man who does not see his own faults is a fallen being; he comes to be so from baseness, turpitude,[1] stupidity and feebleness of intelligence, and lack of discernment and understanding, to such a point that he is no different from vile men and it is not possible to drop lower into degradation than he has. Let him save his soul by seeking out his own faults and turning his

---

[1]   *turpitude*: Base or shameful character; baseness, vileness; depravity, wickedness.

attention to them instead of his pride and the faults of others which do not harm him in this world or the next.[2]

228  I do not know of any benefit to be drawn from hearing about the faults of other people except that he who hears about them may learn the lesson, avoid them, and seek to cure himself of them with Allāh's assistance and might.

229  To speak of the faults of others is a serious shame which is absolutely not acceptable.  One should avoid doing it except when one wishes to advise someone whom one fears to see fall into the clutches of the person who is criticising or when one only wishes to reprimand a boastful person, which should be done to his face and not behind his back.

230  Then you should say to the boastful man, "Turn around and look at yourself. When you have perceived your own faults, you will have found the cure for your pride.  Do not compare yourself with someone who has more faults than you do so that you find it easy to commit faults and imitate wicked people.  [Do not allow yourself to commit vile things and imitate wicked people.]  We have already criticized people who imitate good actions slavishly, what should we say of people who imitate evil actions slavishly?  On the contrary, you should compare yourself with someone who is more virtuous than you, then your pride will fade away.  Then you will be cured of this hateful disease which gave birth in you to scorn of other people when there are without a doubt better people than you among them.  If you scorn them with no cause, they will have cause to scorn you, for the Almighty says, ﴿وَجَزَٰٓؤُا۟ سَيِّئَةٍ سَيِّئَةٌ مِّثْلُهَا...﴾ , «The reward of an evil is an evil like it.»[3] (Quran 42:40) So you will expose yourself to scorn, even to deserved disdain and the anger of Allāh, and the loss of every trace of virtue that there may have been in you.

---

2  ☼ The original translation reads, "…and turning his attention to them instead of his pride and the faults of others, the doing of which harms him neither in this world or the next." I edited it to remove the ambiguity after comparing it with the original Arabic.

3  ☼ The original translation reads, "To condone an evil is to commit the same evil." I checked Source B and Source D but I could not find this phrase in the original Arabic.

231 If you are proud of your intelligence, remember all the bad thoughts that come into your mind and the deceitful hopes which assail you, then you will realize how feeble your intelligence is.

232 If you are proud of your personal ideas, remember your mistakes, keep them in your memory, do not forget them: think of all the times you have believed yourself right and you have been proved wrong, all the times that someone else has been right and you have been wrong. If you do this, you will see that in most cases you have been wrong about as often as right. The score will come out about equal. But it is more likely that your mistakes will be more numerous because this is the case with every human being except the Prophets عليهم السلام!

233 If you are proud of your good works, remember your times of rebellion, your faults, your life in all its aspects. Ah, by Allāh, then you will find that they outnumber your good works and it will make your good deeds forgotten. So you should worry about this for a long time and replace your pride with self-disdain.

234 If you are proud of your knowledge, you should know that it is no credit to you, it is a pure gift that Allāh has granted you. Do not receive it in a way that would anger the Almighty because He might wipe it from you by subjecting you to an illness which would make you forget all that you have learned and stored in your memory. I have been told that this happened to ʿAbd al-Malik ibn Ṭarīf [d. AH 400/1009 CE], who was a scholar, intelligent, moderate, exact in his researches, who had been allotted by fate such a prodigious memory that virtually nothing reached his ears that had to be said to him twice. Now he undertook a journey by ship and experienced such a terrible storm at sea that he lost the memory of most of what he had learnt and suffered considerable upset to his mind. He never recovered his full intelligence. I myself have been struck by illness. When I recovered from it, I had forgotten all my knowledge except for a few ideas of little value. I did not regain it until several years later.

235 You should also know that there are many people greedy for knowledge, who devote themselves to reading, to study, and to research but do not reap

any benefit from it. A scholar should realize that it is enough to pursue knowledge, many others will rank higher than him. Knowledge is truly a gift from Allāh. So what place is there for pride? One can only feel humble, give thanks to Allāh Almighty, and beg Him to increase His gifts and not to withhold them.

236　You should also remember that everything that remains hidden from you, everything that you do not know of the different branches of knowledge, the aspects that you have specialized in, and that you are proud to have penetrated [nevertheless, what you do not know] is greater than what you *do* know. You should therefore replace your pride with scorn and self-disdain, that would be better. Think of those who are more knowledgeable than you – you will find that there are many of them – and may your spirit be humble in your own sight.

237　You should also remember that you may be deceived by knowledge, for if you do not put into practice what you know your knowledge will be a testimony against you and it would have been better for you if you had never been a scholar. For you should remember that an ignorant man is wiser than you, he is in a better position, he is more excusable. May your pride then completely disappear.

238　Moreover, the knowledge that you are so proud of having penetrated is perhaps one of the less important branches of knowledge, of no great value, such as poetry or suchlike. You should then remember the man whose branch of study is more noble than yours on the scale of this world and the next, and your soul should become humble in your own sight.

239　If you are proud of your courage, remember those who are more valiant[4] than you. Then examine what you do with your courage that Allāh has granted you. If you waste it in rebellion against Allāh, you are a fool for you are losing your soul by committing acts of no value to it. If you use your courage in obedience to Allāh, you are spoiling it by your pride. You should

---

[4]　*valiant*: Having or possessing courage; esp. acting with or showing boldness or bravery in fight or on the field of battle; bold, brave, courageous, stout-hearted.

also remember that your courage will fall away as you grow old and if you live so long, you will become dependent, as weak as a baby.

240    It is true that I have never seen less pride than among the brave, and to my mind that proves the purity, greatness, and majesty of their spirits.

241    If you are vain[5] because you are strong, remember those who may rise against you, your peers, your equals, and men who may be perverse, feeble, and vile. But you should remember that they are equal to you in the strength you possess even if you would be ashamed to be like them because of their extreme baseness, ignominy[6] of the souls, their morals, and their origins. You should despise any honours which make you the colleague of such men as I have just described, even if you owned the whole world and you had no opponent – something that is far from likely, since no one has ever heard tell of one man owning the whole inhabited world, even when it was still small and of limited dimensions compared with the uninhabited areas. And just think how tiny it is compared with the celestial sphere that surrounds the universe!

242    Remember what was said by Ibn al-Sammāk [Abū al-ʿAbbās Muḥammad ibn Ṣubayḥ, d. AH 183 / 799 CE] to al-Rashīd when the latter asked to be brought a cup of drinking water: "Commander of the faithful, if you were refused this drink, how much would you offer to get it?"

"My entire kingdom," replied al-Rashīd.

"Commander of the faithful," Ibn al-Sammāk continued, "if you found that you could not pass water (i.e. urine) from you body, how much would you sacrifice to able to do so?"

"My entire kingdom."

---

5   *vain*: Given to or indulging in personal vanity; having an excessively high opinion of one's own appearance, attainments, qualities, possessions, etc.; delighting in, or desirous of attracting, the admiration of others; conceited.
6   *ignominy*: Dishonour, disgrace, shame; infamy; the condition of being in disgrace, etc.

"O Commander of the faithful, how can you boast of a kingdom which is not worth as much as a little urine and a few mouthfuls of water?"[7] Ibn al-Sammāk was right, Allāh grant him peace.

243 If you were king of all the Muslims, you should remember that the king of Sudan, a disreputable black man, an ignorant man who does not cover his private parts, has a larger kingdom than yours. If you say, "I have taken it by right," [no], upon my life, you have not taken it by right if it is a source of arrogance in you and you do not use your position to bring justice. You should be ashamed of your position; it is a state of turpitude,[8] not a state to feel proud of.

244 If you take pride in your wealth, that is the worst degree of pride. Think of all the vile and debauched men who are richer than you and do not take pride in something in which they outdo you. You should realize that it is stupid to take pride in possessions; riches are burdens which bring no benefit until you dispose of them and spend them according to the law. Wealth is also ephemeral and fleeing. It can escape, and you can find it again anywhere, perhaps in someone else's hands, perhaps in the hands of your enemy.[9] To take pride in your wealth is stupid, to put your trust in good fortune is a trap and a weakness.

245 If you take pride in your beauty, think of the harm it gives rise to, which we would be ashamed to put into words. You yourself will be ashamed of it when your beauty disappears with age. But in saying this we have said enough.

---

7  See Ibn Khallikān, *Wafayāt*, vol. 2, p. 296.

8  *turpitude*: Base or shameful character; baseness, vileness; depravity, wickedness.

9  This passage reminds us of Plato's words: "Do not amass gold and silver because the [future] husbands of your [widowed] wives, who will gloat over your demise and ridicule you, will inherit it, while the guilty conscience remains yours alone." [See *Mukhtār min kalām al-Ḥu-kamā' al-Arba'a al-Akābir* in *Dimitri Gutas: Greek Wisdom Literature in Arabic Translation. A study of the Graeco-Arabic Gnomologia* (New Haven: American Oriental Society, 1975), p. 129.

246  If the praises heaped on you by your friends make you vain, think of the criticism that your enemies direct at you. Then your pride will melt away. And if you have no enemies, then you have no good in you at all, for there is nothing lower on the scale of values than the man who has no enemies. That position is reserved for people who have not received from Allāh a single favour worth envying (Allāh preserve us from being in this position!) If you think that your faults are slight, imagine someone else looking at them and think what he would say about them. Then you will feel shame and will know the measure of your faults, if you have the slightest discernment.

247  If you study the laws that regulate human nature and the development of different characters according to the mixture of elements rooted in their souls, you will surely become convinced that you have no merit from your own virtues, that they are only gifts from the Almighty, which, if He had granted to another, would have made him just like you, and you will realize that, left to your own devices, you would collapse and die. You would replace your pride that you take in your virtues with acts of grace towards the One who gave them to you, and with the fear of losing them, for even the most admirable characters can be altered by illness, poverty, fear, anger, or the decrepitude of old age. Show compassion towards those who lack the gifts that you have received, and do not risk losing them by seeking to raise yourself above the One who gave them by claiming merit for yourself or rights in what He has granted to you, or by thinking that you can dispense with His protection, for without it you would perish at once and forever.

248  [For example,] I once suffered a severe illness that caused enlargement of the spleen. I became anguished, peevish, impatient, and touchy, and I reproached myself for this, not being willing to face the fact that my character had changed. I was extremely surprised that I had lost my good characteristics. In this way I had good proof that the spleen is the centre of good temper, and that when it is diseased, bad temper is the result.

249  If you take pride in your ancestry, that is even worse than everything we have mentioned so far, since it is pride in something that has no real usefulness for you in this world or the next. Just ask yourself whether your ancestry

protects you against hunger, or dishonour, or whether it does you any good in the next world.

250   Next, consider those who are equally well descended, or even better, those who are descended from the Prophets عليهم السلام or their successors, from the virtuous companions of Muḥammad or from scholars; then remember those who are descended from non-Arab kings, the Khosrau[10] and Caesars, those who are descended from the Tubbaʿ and the various kings of Islam. Consider what remains of them and what has survived. Observe those who boast of their ancestry as you do of yours, and you will see that most of them are as ignoble as dogs. You will find that they are low, extremely vile, and unreliable; you will find that they are adorned with the very worst of characteristics.

251   Therefore, you should not boast of something in which such people are your equals or even superior to you. The ancestors which make you so proud may have been debauched,[11] drunken, licentious,[12] frivolous,[13] and stupid. Circumstances allowed them to become despots[14] and tyrants; they left an infamous record which will perpetuate their shame for ever. Their crime is immense and their repentance[15] shall be immense on the day of the Last Judgment. Since this is the case, remember that you are taking pride in something that shares in vice, ignominy,[16] shame, and dishonour; it is not something to be admired.

252   If you are proud of your descent from virtuous ancestors, how empty their virtue will leave your hands if you yourself are not virtuous! How little pride your ancestors will have in you in this world and the next if you do no good! All men are children of Ādam whom Allāh created by His own Hand, giving

---

[10] Khosrau or Chosroes is a designation of the ancient Persian kings in general.

[11] *debauched*: Seduced or corrupted from duty or virtue; depraved or corrupt in morals; given up to sensual pleasures or loose living; dissolute, licentious.

[12] *licentious*: Lacking moral discipline or ignoring legal restraint, especially in sexual conduct.

[13] *frivolous*: Unworthy of serious attention; trivial.

[14] *despot*: A person who wields power oppressively; a tyrant.

[15] *repentance*: …sorrow, regret, or contrition for past action or conduct.

[16] *ignominy*: Dishonour, disgrace, shame; infamy; the condition of being in disgrace, etc.

him Paradise for a dwelling place and letting His angels bow down before him. But how little is the advantage they have since all the vices dwell in mankind and all the wicked impious people in the world are among their number.

253 When the wise man considers that the virtues of his ancestors do not bring him any closer to his Lord Almighty and do not win him any favour which he could not have gained by luck in a competition or by his own virtue, not by his wealth, what sense is there in taking pride in a descent which is of no use to him? Someone who feels proud of it, is he not like someone who feels proud of his neighbour's wealth, or a third person's glory, or another's horse because it once wore a bridle that had been his property? It is as people say, "Like a eunuch who takes pride in his father's potency."

254 If your pride leads you to boast, you will be doubly guilty, because your intelligence will have shown that it is incapable of controlling your pride.

255 This would be true if you had a good reason to boast, so imagine what it is like if you have no good reason. Nūḥ's son, Ibrāhīm's father, and Abū Lahab, the uncle of the Prophet – May Allāh grant him blessings, as well Nūḥ and Ibrāhīm – these were the closest relations of Allāh's most virtuous creatures out of all the sons of Ādam. To achieve nobility, it would have been enough to follow in their footsteps. But they drew no benefit from it.

256 Among those who have been born illegitimate, some have risen to the highest positions in control of the world's affairs, e.g. Ziyād [ibn Abīh (d. AH 53/672 CE)] and Abū Muslim al-Khurasānī [d. AH 129/746 CE]. There have been others who have attained supreme virtue, like those whom we respect too highly to name them in this context. We come nearer to Allāh if we love them and model our lives on their glorious achievements.

257 If you take pride in your physical strength, remember that the mule, the donkey, and the bull are stronger than you, and better suited to carrying heavy

loads. If you feel vain[17] about the lightness of your running style, remember that the dog and hare surpass you in this field. It is extremely curious that rational beings feel proud of something in which they are surpassed by dumb animals.

258 You should know that a man who has pride or a feeling of superiority buried deep in his soul should measure how well he tolerates anxieties, adversity, pain, toil, or the worries and misfortunes which plague him. If he realizes that he tolerates them with a bad grace, he should remember that all those who are subjected to trials, those who are starving and have nothing to eat for example, all those who suffer patiently, they have more merit than he does, despite their weaker understanding. However, if he finds that he is capable of endurance, let him remember that this makes him no more exceptional that those we have just mentioned; he may be inferior to them, or their equal, but he is not their superior.

259 Next, let him consider his conduct. Does he act fairly or unfairly when he makes use of the gifts which Allāh has granted him: money, power, slaves, health, or fame? If he finds that he has failed in his obligation to feel grateful towards the Almighty Benefactor, if he finds that he is at the extreme edge of fairness, bordering on injustice, he should remember that people who are just, grateful, and honest have been more favoured than he and are more virtuous than he. If he considers that he does love justice let him remember that a just man is far from being proud because he knows the real importance of things, the real value of characters, and he loves the happy medium which is the balance between two bad extremes; on the contrary, he must incline towards one of these bad extremes.

260 You should remember that if you oppress or maltreat beings whose fate has been entrusted to you by Allāh as slaves or subjects, this shows that you have an ignoble soul, a vile spirit, and a weak intelligence. Indeed, a wise

---

[17] *vain*: Given to or indulging in personal vanity; having an excessively high opinion of one's own appearance, attainments, qualities, possessions, etc.; delighting in, or desirous of attracting, the admiration of others; conceited.

man with his noble spirit, his elevated thoughts, fights only against people as strong as himself, his peers in potency; but to attack those who cannot defend themselves is the sign of a vile nature, a depraved soul and character, it shows you to be incapable and dishonorable. A man who behaved like this would descend to the level of someone who was pleased to have killed a rat, to have exterminated a flea, or to have squashed a louse. There is nothing more base or vile.

261   Remember that it is harder to tame the self than to tame wild beasts. In fact, when wild beasts are shut inside cages ordered for them by kings, they cannot harm you. But the self, even if it were put in a prison, could not be guaranteed to do you no harm.

262   Pride is like a tree trunk; its branches are complacency, presumptuousness,[18] haughtiness,[19] arrogance, and superiority. These terms refer to concepts that are very similar to each other and hard for most people to tell apart. A proud man becomes proud because of an obvious merit: one man may be vain about his own scholarship and be haughty and scornful towards others, another may be vain about his deeds and believe himself to be eminent and superior. One man is proud of his own judgment and becomes arrogant; another is self-satisfied and becomes complacent. Another, full of his own reputation and high standing, becomes self-important and haughty.

263   The lowest degree of pride is when you refrain from laughing when laughter is not out of place; you avoid quick movements and responses except when it is unavoidable in daily life. However, such a fault is very serious. To behave in this way in order to get on with one's work and to avoid time-wasting nonsense would even be a praiseworthy virtue. But these people only behave like this out of disdain for others and from pride in themselves, and so they

---

[18] *presumptuousness*: Characterized by presumption in opinion or conduct; unduly confident or bold; arrogant, presuming; forward, impertinent.

[19] *haughtiness*: High in one's own estimation; lofty and disdainful in feeling or demeanour; proud, arrogant, supercilious. (Of persons, their action, speech, etc.)

deserve only blame, for deeds are of value according to the intentions of the doer, and every being shall be rewarded according to what he intended.[20]

264 Next, a more serious case is when you are not clever enough to keep pride within its rightful limits, when your spirit is too weak, and you reach the point of showing disdain and scorn towards other people by your words and deeds. Then, going even further, when your sense and your spirit are even weaker, you reach the point of desiring to harm people with words and with blows, to give them orders, to commit abuses, to tyrannize them, to exact where possible, obedience and submission from them. When he is unable to do this, the proud man sings his own praises and contents himself with criticizing other people and mocking them.

265 Pride can also exist for no good reason and where there is no merit in the proud person; this is the strangest thing about it. The popular phrase for it is "*Mutamandil* discernment." It is often found in women or in men whose spirit is rather effeminate. It is the pride of someone who has absolutely no good quality: neither knowledge, nor courage, nor high social standing, nor noble descent, nor fortune, which might give him abusive authority.

And, what is more, such a man knows that he is a non-entity in every way, for even the idiot that has stones thrown at him knows this. The only person who can deceive himself is one who has a small part of some good qualities. For example, a man who is endowed with a little brain might imagine himself to have reached the extreme limits of intelligence; someone with a little scientific knowledge might imagine himself to be a perfect expert. Someone whose genealogy has [obscure] bad origins and whose ancestors were not even great tyrants is more infatuated with himself than if he were the son of the [mighty] Pharaoh of the forces.[21] If he has some value as a warrior he thinks he can put 'Alī [ibn Abī Ṭālib] to flight, capture al-Zubayr [ibn al-'Awwām] and slay Khālid [ibn al-Walīd]. If he is at all notorious, he holds Alexander the Great in small esteem. If he is capable of gaining a little

---

[20] This is a part of a *ḥadīth* reported by 'Umar ibn al-Khaṭṭāb and related by al-Bukhārī and Muslim.

[21] This is a Quranic expression. See (Quran 89:10)

money and to obtain a little more than the absolute necessities of life, he is as proud of it as if he had got hold of the sun by its horns. However, pride among such men, even if they are admirable fellows, is not common.

However, it is common among those who have not an iota of knowledge, nobility, fortune, reputation, or courage. They are dragged along by others, and they trample on those who are weaker than themselves. Although they are perfectly aware that they themselves are lacking in all good qualities and have none whatsoever, they are still haughty and insolent.

266   I took the opportunity of asking one such man – gently and tactfully – what was the cause of his sense of superiority and his disdain of others. The only answer I could get was this: "I am a free man," he said, "I am nobody's slave."

I replied, "Most people that one meets share this same quality with you. Like you, they are free men, except for a certain number of slaves who are more generous than you and who give orders to you and to many other free men." I could not get anything else out of him.

267   I returned to consideration of their case, going into the matter deeply. I thought about it for years on end, trying to find the reasons which drove them to pride that was so unjustified. I searched the recesses of their souls incessantly, on the basis of what their words reflected of their situation and their intentions. I came to the conclusion that they imagined themselves to have a superior intelligence and perception and a good sense of judgment. [They believed that] if fate had allowed them to make use of these talents, they would have had immense possibilities, they would have known how to direct powerful kingdoms, and their merit would have appeared superior to that of other men. If they had a fortune, they would have been very good at spending it. And this is the angle by which vanity has taken possession of them and pride has penetrated their souls.

268   Here one might make curious digressions and [point out] certain paradoxes. It is a fact that no virtue except that of intelligence and perception allows one to believe that one is a past master in it, and the more one is completely sure that one has attained perfection in it, the more one lacks it.

This is so much the case that one will see a raving lunatic or an inveterate sot[22] making fun of a sane man. A mentally deficient person will mock men who are wise, virtuous, and knowledgeable. Little boys shout after grown men. Men who are stupid and insolent disdain men who are intelligent and reserved. Even the weakest women think that the spirit and opinions of great men lack vigour. In sum, the weaker the intelligence the more man imagines himself well endowed and in possession of excellent powers of perception. This is not at all the case with other qualities: someone who has none of them knows that he lacks them. Error only arises in a man who has a small portion, even if it is tiny, because he then imagines – if he has limited powers of perception – that he possesses this quality to the highest degree.

269 The cures for pride among such people are poverty and obscurity; there is nothing more effective, for if not awed,[23] they are bad and a considerable nuisance to other men. You find them doing nothing but discrediting people, attacking their reputations, mocking at everybody, scorning all rights, and permitting themselves every indiscretion. They go to the limit, to the point of risking injury to themselves, and entering into dispute. They even come to blows and punches for the most futile cause that presents itself.

270 It can happen that pride lies hidden in the depths of a man's heart and does not appear until he meets with some success or acquires some fortune and his good sense can neither control nor conceal this feeling.

271 Something that I have seen that is very curious – among certain weak creatures – is that they are so dominated by a deep love for their grandchild or their wife that they describe them in public as extremely intelligent. They go as far as to say, "She is more intelligent than me and I regard her advice as a blessing." They praise her beauty, her charm, her vivacity[24] – this often happens with very feeble men – and do it so much and so well that if they

---

[22] *inveterate*: Of evil feelings, prejudices, and the like.

  *sot*: A foolish or stupid person; a fool, blockhead, dolt.

[23] *awed*: Influenced by dread or reverence; awe-struck.

[24] *vivacity*: Intellectual or mental animation, acuteness, or vigour; quickness or liveliness of conception or perception.

wished to find her a husband they need say nothing more in order to make someone desire her from their description. Such behaviour is only found among souls which are weak and lacking in all self-esteem.

272 Take care not to boast, because nobody will believe you, even if you are telling the truth. On the contrary, they will take everything that you have said when boasting about yourself and use it as the basis of their criticism of you.

273 Take care not to praise someone to his face; this would be to behave like a vile flatterer.

274 Also take care not to pretend to be poor. You will not gain anything except to be treated as a liar or to be scorned by anyone who listens to you. You will have no benefit from it except that you will fail to recognize the gifts you have from the Lord, and if you complain about it to anyone they will have no pity on you.

275 You should also take care not to display your wealth, for all that you will achieve is that those who hear you will covet what you possess.

276 Be content to offer thanks to the Almighty, to confide your needs to Him, and to take notice of those who are inferior to Him. In this way you will keep your dignity, and those who envy you will leave you alone.

277 A wise man is one who does not neglect the duties imposed upon him by intelligence.

278 Anyone who tempts others with his riches has no choice but to share them out – and there would be no end to this – or to refuse them which would make him seem mean and would attract universal hostility. If you wish to give something to somebody, do it of your own initiative and before he asks for it; this is more noble, more disinterested and more worthy of praise.

279 Something peculiar about envy is when you hear a jealous person say, when someone has done original work in some branch of science, "What a silly person! Nobody has ever put forward that hypothesis before and nobody

has ever believed that." But if the same person hears someone expound an idea which is not new, he exclaims, "What a silly person! This is not a new idea!" This sort of person is harmful because he is bent on obstructing the path of knowledge and turning people away from it in order to increase the number of his own sort, the ignorant.

280 The wisdom of the wise man brings him no profit in the eyes of a wicked man; the latter thinks that he is as wicked as himself. Thus I have seen vile creatures imagine in their vile souls that everybody was like themselves; they would never believe that it was possible, in one way or another, not to have their faults. There is no character more corrupt; there is none more remote from being virtuous and good. Anyone who is in this state cannot hope to be cured at all. Allāh help us in all matters.

281 Justice is a fortress in which all who are frightened take refuge. In fact, if a tyrant feels oppressed, does he not call for justice and scorn and condemn injustice? But you never see the opposite, someone condemning justice. Therefore a man who is equitable by nature can rest at peace in this impregnable fortress.

282 Scorn is a variety of treachery, for someone can be disloyal towards you without scorning you, but if he scorns you he is betraying the impartiality he should show towards you. Therefore every scornful man is disloyal, but not every disloyal man is scornful.

283 If you scorn a thing it shows that you scorn the man who possesses it.

284 There are two circumstances in which it is good to do something which would otherwise be bad: it is when one wishes to reproach someone or to present excuses to someone. In these two cases, it is permissible to list past benefits and recall gifts. In all cases except these two, it would be in the worst possible taste.

285 We should not criticise someone who has a natural tendency towards a vice – even if it were the worst possible fault, the greatest of vices – as long as he does not let it appear in anything he says or does. He would almost

deserve more commendation than someone who naturally inclines towards virtue, for it takes a strong and virtuous mind to control a corrupt natural inclination.

286  To attack a man's conjugal honour is worse than to attack his life.

287  To a well-born man, honour is dearer than gold.  A well-born man should use his gold to protect his body, his body to protect his soul, his soul to protect his honour, and his honour to defend his religion.  But he must never sacrifice his religion in defense of anything whatsoever.

288  To attack a man's honour is less serious than to steal from his property.  The proof of this is that almost nobody, not even the most virtuous, can say that he has never attacked anyone's honour, though it may have been only rarely.  But to have stolen someone's property, whether on a small scale or a large scale, is definitely the deed of a vile person and far from virtue.

289  Drawing analogies between different situations is mostly deceptive and it can be quite false.  This form of argument is not acceptable in problems which concern religion.

290  A man who blindly follows another slavishly is asking to be cheated out of his own thoughts when he would consider it the greatest crimes to be cheated out of his money.  He is equally wrong in both cases.

291  A man who considers it hateful to be tricked out of his fortune, and regards it as the worst of crimes, must have an ignoble character, a mean spirit, and a soul worthy of disdain.

292  Anyone who does not know where to find virtue should rely on the commandments of Allāh and His Prophet  .  All the virtues are contained in these commandments.

293  It is possible to bring about something dangerous by trying to guard against it.  It is possible to let out a secret by trying hard to keep it.  Sometimes it is better to avoid a subject than to raise doubts by dwelling on it.  In

each of these cases the harm comes from overdoing it and going beyond the boundaries of the happy medium.

294 Virtue is the medium between the two extremes [the "too much" and the "too little"]. These two extremes are to be criticised – and virtue, lying between them, is to be praised – except when it is a question of intelligence, and then there can be no excess.

295 It is better to sin by being too strict than by being too soft.

296 It is astonishing to see that virtue is regarded as lovely but difficult, and vice as awful but easy to commit.

297 A person who wishes to be fair should put himself in his adversary's position. He will then see the unfairness of his own behaviour.

298 The definition of strictness consists of being able to distinguish friend from foe. The height of stupidity and weakness is the inability to distinguish one's foe from one's friend.

299 Do not deliver your enemy to an oppressor, and do not oppress him yourself. Treat him as you would treat your friend, except for trusting him. Be careful not to mix with him or help him rise socially; that would be the behaviour of a fool. Anyone who treats his enemy as equal to his friend in closeness and in promoting his position only succeeds in making people avoid his friendship and they find it just as easy to be his enemies. He will only win the disrespect of his enemy by handing him his vulnerable places, and he will lose his friend, since the latter will join the ranks of his adversaries.

300 The greatest of good deeds is to refrain from punishing your enemy and from handing him over to an oppressor. As for mixing with him, that is the mark of fools who will soon be lost.

301 The worst evil is to oppress your friend. As for keeping him away from yourself, that would be the action of a man without spirit and destined to misfortune.

302　Magnanimity[25] consists not of mingling with your enemies but of showing mercy to them while still not trusting them.

304　How many men have we seen take pride in their possessions and so be lost!  Guard against this attitude, it is really harmful and completely useless.  How many men we have seen lost because of something they said.  But we have never heard of anyone being lost because he kept silent.  Therefore you should speak only to please your Creator; and if you fear that what you say will be abused, then keep silent.

305　I have rarely seen a lost opportunity ever reoccur.

306　A man undergoes many trials during his life, but the worst are those inflicted by his fellow man.  The harm done by man to man is worse than the harm done by furious beasts and poisoned vipers for you can protect yourself against animals, but you cannot protect yourself at all against the human race.

307　Hypocrisy is the thing which is most widespread among people.  Despite this, it is amazing to see that people only like those who treat them hypocritically.

308　If we said that characters are round like a globe because their extremes meet, we should not be far from the truth.  Indeed we see that the consequences of the two extremes are alike and a person cries for joy as much as he cries for sorrow; too much love makes one commit as many successive faults as excessive hatred does, and can cause estrangement if the loved one lacks patience and fairness.

309　If a man is dominated by a natural passion, then however firm and sensible he is in other ways, he can be overcome if you attack this weak point.

310　An over-suspicious mind learns to tell lies.  Since he often needs to excuse himself by lying, he is practised in it and finds it easy.

---

[25] *magnanimity*: Nobility of feeling; superiority to petty resentment or jealousy; generous disregard of injuries.

311  The most impartial witness against a man who is given to sincerity is his face; it clouds over as soon as he tells a lie or is about to do so.

312  The most implacable[26] witness against a liar is his own tongue; it gets twisted and contradicts itself.

313  It is a greater catastrophe to have an unfaithful friend than to lose him.

314  Those who show most horror when speaking out loud of shameful acts are those who are most apt to commit them. This can clearly be seen in the insolence offered by guttersnipes[27] and the insults of vile men who have reached the nadir[28] of vileness in practising vile professions. For example, those men and women who earn a living by playing the flute, sweeping out farmyards, working as servants in abattoirs, and those who frequent the [drinking houses] brothel, authorized as meeting places of people of the lowest class or stable boys. Nobody abuses them more than they abuse themselves. More than anybody else they cry scandal when they wallow[29] in it in the first place and have acquired the worst of reputations by it.

315  Meetings make grudges melt away.[30] One would think that when glances meet, hearts grow peaceful. Do not torture yourself if your friend meets your enemy, for the meeting will lessen the latter's hatred towards you.

316  The worst misfortunes that can come upon men are fear, anxiety, sickness, and poverty. But the thing that makes the soul suffer most cruelty is the anxiety of losing what one loves and to see something happen that one hates. After this comes sickness, then fear, then poverty. The proof of this is that people would willingly accept poverty to avoid the pains of illness. For a man quests ardently after health and does not count what he spends to recover it when he fears death. When his end is certain he would like to be able to give his entire fortune to be saved and cured. Fear is bearable when it drives off

---

[26] *implacable*: That cannot be appeased; irreconcileable; inexorable: of persons, feelings, etc.

[27] *guttersnipe*: A child brought up 'in the gutter'; one of the lowest class; an urchin.

[28] *nadir*: The lowest point (of anything); the place or time of greatest depression or degradation.

[29] *wallow*: To roll the body about indolently or clumsily in or as if in water, snow, or mud.

[30] This is a part of a *ḥadīth*. ✿ In my brief research, I could not find this narration.

anxiety, for a man seeks with all his soul to drive away anxiety. The worst of all illnesses is pain that persists in one organ, always the same.

317   But to be a well-born spirit, humiliation is less bearable than all the misfortunes we have described.  On the other hand, it is the one that knavish[31] spirits fear the least.

---

[31] *knavish*: Roguish, rascally, mischievous, impertinent.

Chapter Eleven

# *Characteristics of the Soul*

318 A wise man should not judge by appearances when a sniveller[1] cries for mercy, pretends that he is oppressed, complains, twists and turns, and laments. With a man who behaves like this I have become certain that he was the oppressor who went over the limit and committed excessive abuses. And likewise I have seen a man bearing an injustice speak calmly without complaining and only displaying a little anxiety. At first glance, without further examination, you would have taken him for the oppressor. In cases such as this it is important to establish the facts, fight resolutely against our inclination to take sides, not incline towards or against such attitudes as we have described, and seek to be impartial to all, as we are obliged to by justice.

319 A curious thing about human nature is that carelessness is bad when it is good to know how to make use of it sometimes. This can only be explained by the fact that a man who is naturally inclined to carelessness makes use of it when he should be vigilant. It is absentmindedness with no sense of reality. His carelessness belongs under the heading of ignorance and that is why it is bad. On the other hand, a spirit which is vigilant by nature only makes use of carelessness for a good purpose when he should not study or research deeply into the subject. To pretend to ignore something in this case means to understand reality, to refuse to act precipitously,[2] to use moderation, and to prevent the worst happening. Thus it is praiseworthy to know how to pretend not to be listening and bad to be naturally inattentive.

---

[1] *snivel*: To make a sniffing or snuffling sound expressive of real or assumed emotion; to be in, or affect, a tearful state.

[2] *precipitious*: Involving risk of sudden fall or ruin.

320  The same could be said about admitting one is afraid or concealing fact. To make it obvious that one is troubled as soon as one begins to have difficulties is bad, because it means that you cannot control yourself and your display of emotion serves no useful purpose. Indeed, divine law counsels against it; it stops you doing what has to be done and to make the necessary arrangements in view of the events which one foresees and which may be more terrible than the present situation which has given rise to this fear.

321  Now, given that it is wrong to let your fear be seen, the opposite is good, that is, to display patience, because that means you are in control of yourself, you have turned away from useless actions and towards actions which are profitable and useful both immediately and in the future.

322  As for hiding your patience, that is wrong too, since it would look as if you were unfeeling, hardhearted and lacking in mercy. These faults are found only among wicked people, vicious natures, and cruel and vile souls.

323  All this being very ugly, the opposite, which consists of concealing the fact that you are troubled, is praiseworthy because it is a mark of piety, gentleness, charity, and compassion.

324  Thus one can say that the happy medium, for a man, is to have a sensitive soul but an impassive[3] body, that is to say that neither on his face nor in his comportment[4] should there be any sign that he is troubled.

If a man whose own judgment is poor only knew what harm his false calculations had brought upon him so far, he would find success in the future if he stopped relying on his own judgment. Allāh guide us.

---

[3]  *impassive*: Deficient in, or void of, mental feeling or emotion; not susceptible to mental impressions; unimpressionable, apathetic; also, in good sense, not liable to be disturbed by passion, serene.

[4]  *comportment*: Personal bearing, carriage, demeanour, deportment; behaviour, outward conduct, course of action.

Chapter Twelve

# *Man's Desire to Know*

325   There are longings from which hardly anyone is exempt, except a man whose thoughts are completely vile or one who has trained himself by a perfect system of discipline and has completely tamed the power of his angry soul. In order to cure the avid desire that the soul feels to seize information that one wants to conceal from it or to see an object that one wants to hide from it, you should think of all the things of the same kind which escape it in places where it has not been, let alone the most distant areas of the earth. If the person worries about them he is completely mad and totally lacking in reason. [On the other hand] if he is not worried about these other things, is the thing hidden from him not the same as these things that do not worry him, absolutely identical in fact? He should multiply the arguments directed against his passion, and he should speak to his soul with the voice of reason, "O my soul, if you did not know that there was something there being hidden from you, do you think that you would worry about getting to know it?" There is no doubt that the answer would be "No." Then he should say to his soul, "Act as if you did not know that there was something there being hidden from you. Then you can relax and you will be able to drive away your anxiety and calm your painful agitation and your hateful greed." These are numerous victories, considerable gains, and noble ambitions to which a wise man aspires and which only someone totally lacking disdains.

326   As for the man who has the ambition and the obsession to spread his fame to every country and to be remembered throughout the centuries, let him reflect and say to his soul, "O my soul, if you were gloriously famous in all the countries of the world for all eternity and to the end of time, but

if I was not told about it and if I knew nothing about it, do you think I would be happy or satisfied about it, yes or no?" There is no doubt that the answer would be "No," for any other answer would be impossible. Having convinced himself of this truth, the man must understand that when he is dead he will have no possibility of knowing whether he is famous or not. Moreover he would not know while he was still alive if nobody told him.

327 He should also consider two important points. First, that there have been in earlier times a great number of virtuous Prophets and Messengers of Allāh عليهم السلام of whom nobody on the surface of the earth remembers their name, nor their history, nor their trace, nor any memory, nor the slightest thing about them.

328 Second, there have been, among the good and virtuous men who were the companions of the Prophets in ancient times, ascetics, philosophers, scholars, excellent men, kings of nations which have disappeared, founders of cities which are now deserted, and courtesans of princes whose history has also not reached us. Nobody knows anything about them nowadays and nobody has the slightest knowledge that they existed. Has this fact harmed any of them? Has it diminished their merit and destroyed their good deeds? Has it lowered them in the eyes of their Almighty Creator? Let me tell anyone who did not already know it, that there does not exist anywhere in the world the smallest scrap of information about any of the earthly sovereigns or the ancient generations who preceded men's historical knowledge, which begins with the kings of Isrā'īl. And everything that we know of the history of the sovereigns of Greece and of Persia does not go back further than two thousand years. Where is the remembrance of the men who peopled the earth before them? Is it not, in fact, totally wiped out, vanished, forgotten?

This is why the Almighty has spoken of ﴿رُسُلًا لَّمْ نَقْصُصْهُمْ عَلَيْكَ﴾ «Messengers of whom We have not told you the history at all,» (Quran 4:164) and Allāh also said, ﴿وَقُرُونًا بَيْنَ ذَلِكَ كَثِيرًا ٢٨﴾ «Many centuries in between,» (Quran 25:38) and Allāh also said, ﴿وَالَّذِينَ مِنْ بَعْدِهِمْ لَا يَعْلَمُهُمْ إِلَّا اللَّهُ﴾ «Those who came after and who are known only to Allāh.» [Quran 14:9] Even if the memory of a man persists for a short period of time, would that in itself make him any different from those who lived in olden times in nations that have disappeared and of which the memory also persisted a short while before being completely lost?

329 We should also think of those who were famous for their good deeds or their bad deeds; did their fame raise them one single degree in the sight of Allāh? Did it win them a reward that they had not already won by their actions during their life?

330 Since this is not so,[1] the desire to be famous is nothing but the desire for something absolutely senseless and useless. On the contrary, a wise man should aspire only to multiply his virtues and good deeds, which make the one who applies himself to them merit a good reputation, praise, commendation, and a praiseworthy reputation which will bring him nearer to his Creator and will be useful in remembering him to the Almighty. He will keep himself in this beneficial state and will never be lost for all eternity; assistance is from Allāh.

331 Gratitude towards a benefactor is a necessary obligation. To fulfill it, you should at least render to him the good that he had done to you and more. Afterwards, you should show interest in his affairs, protect him as much as possible, faithfully keep to promises you have made him, in his life or after his death, and to his relations, both distant and close. Thus you should continue to show affection to him, to give him advice. You should make his good qualities known truthfully and you should conceal his faults. [These obligations lie upon you] for the rest of your life and should be handed down to your descendents and to those you love.

332 However, it is no part of gratitude to assist someone in committing sin and not advise him in cases where he is doing himself harm in this world and the next. On the contrary, anyone who helps his benefactor to do evil is deceiving him, denying his benefactions, acting unjustly in his respect, and failing to recognize his goodness. Moreover, the bounties and benefactions

---

[1] ☼ The original translation reads, "Since this is so..." This seemed incorrect since the author رحمه الله is referring to the two rhetorical questions in the previous paragraph, i.e. since their fame does NOT rise, and since it does NOT win them a reward. Allāh knows best.

of Allāh towards each one of His creatures are much more considerable, more longstanding, and more salutary than those of any other benefactor. Indeed, it is the Almighty who has opened our eyes to see, who has pierced our ears to hear, it is He who has granted us the other excellent senses and has endowed us with speech and discernment, two benefits by grace of which we have been made able to hear His words. He has subjected to our service everything which exists in the skies and upon the earth – stars and elements – and has placed none of His creatures above us, except only His holy angels, the inhabitants of the heavens. What are the gifts of men compared with these! Anyone who imagines that he is thanking a benefactor by helping him to do evil, or by taking his side when he should not, would be denying the gifts of the greatest of his benefactors, whose gifts he would be failing to recognize. He would not be rendering thanks to Him, to whom all thanks truly belong, he would not be praising Him who is the essence of praiseworthiness, that is to say, Allāh Almighty.

Anyone who steps between his benefactor and evil, leading him back to the bitter truth, would be showing true gratitude and would be fulfilling perfectly his obligation towards him. Praises be to Allāh at first and at last and in all circumstances!

Chapter Thirteen

# *Attending Study-Sessions*

333    If you attend a study-session, behave only like someone who wishes to increase his knowledge and to win greater recompense from Allāh. Do not behave like someone who is content with what he has, who is looking for some fault to criticise or a curious detail to hawk around. This would be the behaviour of vile men who never succeed in their studies.

If you come to it with good intentions, you will always obtain the best results. Otherwise, to stay at home would be less tiring for your body, more worthy of your moral conduct, and more salutary[1] for your religious life.

334    If you do attend under the conditions that we have indicated, take care to adopt one of these three attitudes and there cannot be a fourth: [First,] you may keep quiet in the silence of ignorance. Thus you will obtain the reward of your intention in attending the study-session, praise for your reserve, dignity in your behaviour and the friendship of those you mix with.

335    [Second,] if you do not behave like this, ask the questions which someone who wished to learn would ask. Then you will obtain, in addition to the four advantages just mentioned, a fifth, which is to increase your knowledge. What characterises the questions asked by someone who wishes to learn is that he only asks about the points he does not know, not those he does know. To ask about what one already knows is a proof of ineptitude and a

---

[1]    *salutary*: Conducive to well-being; calculated to bring about a more satisfactory condition, or to remedy some evil; beneficial, 'wholesome.'

weak spirit, it is only palaver[2] and a useless waste of time for oneself and for others. By doing this you will only provoke dislike and it will only be pure verbiage. So do not play games, it is a bad fault.

If the person you are asking replies satisfactorily, stop questioning. If his reply is not satisfactory, or if you do not understand it, say to him, "I do not understand," and ask him to elaborate. If he does not explain himself more clearly, if he keeps silent or if he repeats what he said before without adding anything, keep silent, otherwise you will only bring upon yourself trouble and dislike, without obtaining the desired enlightenment.

336 [Third,] you can riposte[3] as a scholar would, that is to say that you can reply to the arguments advanced in a way that refutes them clearly. If you are not capable of replying in this way, if you are able only to repeat yourself or to reply using arguments which your adversary will not find convincing, do not insist for you will not gain by your repetitions any extra result or any information. You will only succeed in annoying yourself and starting a hostility between the two of you which could have serious consequences.

337 Guard against the questions that a prejudiced man would ask and the ripostes of a show-off who is bent on being right without knowing anything about the matter. These two attitudes are bad: they witness to absence of piety, a great tendency to verbiage, a weakness of spirit and considerable vanity. Let us commend the matter to Allāh who is our best support.

338 If certain statements are put to you verbally, or if you come across a written text, guard against reacting violently, which will bring about excesses in language, before you have assured yourself by irrefutable proof that the ideas expressed are erroneous.

Neither should you accept them with the enthusiasm of someone who is credulous[4] and convinced until you have assured yourself of their veracity

---

[2] *palaver*: Applied contemptuously to (what is considered) unnecessary, profuse, or idle talk; 'jaw.'

[3] *riposte*: To reply or retaliate; to answer (one).

[4] *credulous*: Over-ready to believe; apt to believe on weak or insufficient grounds.

by an irrefutable proof. In the two cases, you would be shutting your eyes and turning away from knowing the truth. On the contrary, consider what is being put to you as one who is neither against it nor for it or one who wants to understand would, to the best of his ability, what he has heard and read in order to increase his knowledge, to adopt the new ideas if they are good or reject them if they are erroneous. It is certain that if you behave like this you will be generally rewarded, greatly praised, and your merit will be recognized.

339 A man who is content with the small fortune that he has and does not envy your opulence[5] is as rich as you, even if you are a Croesus. If this man resists the bait of gain to which you have succumbed, he will be much richer than you.

340 Anyone who rises above the things of this world to which you kneel is mightier than you.

341 It is a pious duty for Muslims to teach the good and to practise it. Anyone who does both these things at once is doing two virtuous deeds to perfection. But a person who contents himself with teaching the good without practicing it is acting well by teaching and acting badly by failing to put his teaching into practise, so mingling a good with a bad deed. This case is preferable to that of the person who would not teach the good any more than he would practise it. Such a man, although not virtuous, is more worthy of imitation, he is less blameworthy than someone who forbids the teaching of good and opposes anyone who practises it.

342 If it was only a man completely without sin who had the right to forbid evil, if it was only the man of perfect virtue who could teach the good, nobody yet would have forbidden evil or ordained the good since [the death of] the Prophet ﷺ. This should be enough to make clear to you the corruption, wickedness, and opprobrium[6] of anyone who might think this.

---

[5] *opulence*: Wealth, riches, affluence.

[6] *opprobrium*: The disgrace or evil reputation attached to conduct considered shameful; the imputation or expression of this disgrace; infamy, reproach.

343 Abū Muḥammad رضي الله عنه said, "Here someone contradicted, protesting, 'When al-Ḥasan [al-Baṣrī] رضي الله عنه forbade something [bad], he never did it himself, and when he ordained something [good], he himself put his orders firmly into practice. Wisdom requires that we do the same, for it has been said that: nothing is more odious than to preach something and not practise it, or to preach against an action and then to do it.' "

344 Abū Muḥammad replied, "The person who said that was lying. There is something more ugly, that is, not to preach good and not to preach against evil and also to allow oneself to act badly and not to do good."

345 Abū Muḥammad added, "Abū al-Aswad al-Duʿalī said,[7]

Do not forbid a vice that you are given to yourself
    for great shame will fall on you.
Start with yourself and forbid yourself your own misdeeds.
    If you stop devoting yourself to them you will become wise.
Then your sermons will be accepted, people will take example
    from your knowledge and your teaching will be profitable.' "

346 Abū Muḥammad continued, Abū al-Aswad wished to condemn only someone who has done a deed after forbidding it to others: such a deed would be doubly bad for having been committed by the very person who forbade it. The poet was quite right for this is what the Almighty said, ﴿أَتَأْمُرُونَ ٱلنَّاسَ بِٱلْبِرِّ وَتَنسَوْنَ أَنفُسَكُمْ﴾ «Will you command people to do good and forget to do it yourself?» (Quran 2:44). It cannot be believed that Abū al-Aswad wanted to express any other idea. As for thinking that he did not want to be condemned for a bad deed, Allāh protect him from that! That would have been to act like a wicked man.

347 Here is a true story about al-Ḥasan. When he heard someone say that only a person who did no evil had the right to forbid evil, he replied, "Shayṭān would like us to believe that, and then nobody could forbid evil or ordain

---

7 ✪ I made slight edits here to cater for margin constraints while maintaining meaning.

good." Abū Muḥammad continued, "Al-Ḥasan was right, and that is what we said before."

348  May Allāh grant that we may be counted among those whom He permits to do good and to practice it, and among those who see the straight road, for no one is without faults; someone who perceives his own weaknesses will forget those of others. May Allāh permit us to die on the Sunnah [law] of Muḥammad. Āmīn, O Lord of the Worlds!

[This book is finished, by the Grace of Allāh, His help, and His good will. May Allāh bless our master Muḥammad, his family, and his companions, grant them life eternal, and may Allāh be pleased with Aḥmad [Muḥammad], Messenger of Allāh!]

9 789394 834330